Walking on Our Sacred Path

Critical Indigenous and American Indian Studies

Andrew Jolivette
General Editor

Vol. 6

The Critical Indigenous and American Indian Studies series
is part of the Peter Lang Humanities list.
Every volume is peer reviewed and meets
the highest quality standards for content and production.

PETER LANG
New York • Berlin • Brussels • Lausanne • Oxford

Walking on Our Sacred Path

Indigenous American Women Affirming Identity and Activism

Edited by Isabel Dulfano

PETER LANG
New York • Berlin • Brussels • Lausanne • Oxford

Library of Congress Cataloging-in-Publication Data

Names: Dulfano, Isabel, editor.
Title: Walking on our sacred path: indigenous American women affirming identity and activism / Isabel Dulfano.
Other titles: Indigenous American women affirming identity and activism
Description: New York: Peter Lang, 2023.
Series: Critical indigenous and American Indian studies; vol. 6
ISSN 2376-547X (print) | ISSN 2376-5488 (online)
Includes bibliographical references and index.
Identifiers: LCCN 2022032196 (print) | LCCN 2022032197 (ebook)
ISBN 978-1-4331-9737-6 (hardback) | ISBN 978-1-4331-9738-3 (paperback)
ISBN 978-1-4331-9739-0 (ebook pdf) | ISBN 978-1-4331-9740-6 (epub)
Subjects: LCSH: Indian women activists–North America–Interviews. | Indian women activists–South America–Interviews. | Indian women–Attitudes. | Indian women–Political activity. | Indians of North America–Ethnic identity. | Indians of South America–Ethnic identity.
Classification: LCC E98.W8 W26 2023 (print) | LCC E98.W8 (ebook) | DDC 305.48/897–dc23/eng/20220707
LC record available at https://lccn.loc.gov/2022032196
LC ebook record available at https://lccn.loc.gov/2022032197
DOI 10.3726/b20036

Bibliographic information published by **Die Deutsche Nationalbibliothek**. **Die Deutsche Nationalbibliothek** lists this publication in the "Deutsche Nationalbibliografie"; detailed bibliographic data are available on the Internet at http://dnb.d-nb.de/.

For Shoshana, Maia Raquel, Aliastra, Isaac and Luise

Table of Contents

Foreword

The primary objective of this book is to present in formal published form Indigenous women's voices as they speak of their identity and activism. When I conducted the interviews, between 2016 and 2018, the women who spoke to me granted permission for video and/or audio recordings. Verbatim transcriptions were made, translated into English when necessary. The transcriptions were returned to each woman for review, approval, and consent for use in a published document. In one case, an interviewee made extensive editorial changes to her transcribed text. Others made minor factual, contextual or spelling corrections. I did not edit any of the text transcriptions. The collection of transcribed interviews appeared online in pdf format, in the version approved by each woman.

As I sought the publication of these interviews as a book manuscript, it was suggested by multiple readers that, beyond exclusive transcription of the interviews, I develop a critical discussion of the themes that emerged from the interviews as a whole, and embed passages from each one. With this publication of these excerpts, the publisher requested, from each interviewee, a signed release of liability and rights to the distribution of the contributor's comments. In this instance, some preferred to remain unnamed, withholding renewed consent to use their identities.

Across industries and sectors of our society and business concerns, the balance of power has been, and continues to be, abused to the detriment of Native Peoples. Examples abound in every field as appropriation and exploitation remain unchecked. Publication within academic settings is no exception. In the publication of this book, these issues came into play.

Historically, Native women's names have been omitted or erased from European and White Settler discussion regarding the Indigenous. In some cases, a woman might choose to have her name omitted from these discussions. There is often peril in being named. In many cases, a woman is forced to be silent. In some instances, a woman chooses to remain anonymous as an act of political defiance against sectors and industries which, proforma, appropriate her identity. And, in other situations, a woman chooses to speak out, with her name and identity front and center.

My intent is not to violate the expressed preferences of the interviewees in the manner in which their voices are heard. In the spirit of this professed intention, and to honor the rights of these women to control their own voices and identities, I have had to omit some names and/or to offer generalized profiles in the use of some of the interview extracts. Although some of the women I interviewed have withdrawn entirely from being presented in this book, I bring, as much as possible, the gist and eloquence of their articulations regarding the challenges and realities represented in this book. Attribution of a credible source is a key ingredient to ethical writing. It is unfortunate that not all of the information about the voices here are revealed. A name brings a stronger story to the reader. However, respect for the choices made by each of these women is of greater import.

Interviewing these women, then negotiating with them and a publisher, has been an exercise in decolonization for me. From the organization of the interview content to the extensive international web of collaboration to agreements in oral and written form to bringing the voices of these women onto the printed page, I was forced to confront myself in regard to appropriation. I had to consider the ubiquitous structural centers of power that might impede their self-representation. Collaborations meant to be deployed in the public arena require questions regarding the control of knowledge production. On virtual platforms such as social media sites, content is often censored or can be deleted. I have had to look hard at my own fissures to see where I must delete, reconfigure, or release information about some of the participants.

Preface

I have had some interesting life experiences in my many years of advocacy and fighting for survival and social justice for my people. When Isabel asked me to write this preface for the book, I was taken a bit by surprise as I felt I hadn't had the experience as many Women Leaders do in the Southern Continent. Perhaps that's what makes my contribution a bit different and I hope valuable to some extent. I hope what I share will be helpful to those women leaders who fight the good fight every single day of their lives. Women Leaders are the heart of their communities and they will be the ones who find the pathway to survival for their people.

> "A nation is not conquered until the hearts of its women are on the ground. Then it is finished, No matter how brave its warriors or how strong their weapons."
> Cheyenne proverb

I am a member of the Penobscot Indian Nation, a small tribe located in the State of Maine, the northeastern-most state in the United States. There are five tribes in Maine, each tribe numbering around 2,000 members more or less. Together these tribes are referred to as Wabanaki Tribes. Wabanaki meaning people of the Dawnland. The tribes have been kept in poverty since Maine became a State in 1820. We all have a long and traditional history of joining the United States

Military. The military has always been a way for each individual Tribal Member to escape from the communities that have been kept in poverty. It has also been a way for us to protect what's left of our homeland. The military provided us with jobs, education and a way to travel and see the rest of the world. Not all Tribal Members chose that path, but I was one who did. I joined the Women's Army Corp in 1966 and was sent to Vietnam in 1968. Since my service in Vietnam I have held positions in Law Enforcement as the Police Chief with Penobscot Nation, Director of Security at Bowdoin College, Multicultural Director at the University of Southern Maine and represented the Penobscot Nation in the Maine State Legislature for twelve years. I am now retired and am a member of our Tribal Council. I have learned important lessons from each position I've held. I will say that the most memorable experience I've had in my close to 70 years on this earth is the experience of being in a war.

My father and uncles were all veterans, my father from WWII, my uncles the Korean War. I heard all these stories that intrigued me. The horror of war never registered in my brain. I was determined to go to Vietnam even though at that time no women were allowed in combat. I ended up going as a Communication Specialist. I handled all the casualty reports for South East Asia. I was there during the TET Offensive. I realized a few years later after I returned home and had been on a return visit to Vietnam in 1995 that I, as a soldier in the Army, invaded that culture just as the Europeans invaded mine. I have been asked why would your people join the military of a Country that is trying to eliminate you? A very fair question. I think to understand why one needs to know something about our history. I will just give a brief example.

On June 21, 1775, Chief Joseph Orono (my great grandfather seven times removed) addressed the Penobscot warriors just before they were to participate in the American Revolution with these words:

> The Great Spirit gives us freely all things. Our white brothers tell us they came to Indian country to enjoy liberty and life but a Great Saga is coming to bind them in chains, to kill them. We must fight him for should he bind them in bonds, next he will treat us like bears. He will tear away from us Indian liberties and land. We must help his ill-treated sons for they will return good for good and the law of love runs through their children…
>
> Look down the stream of time. Look up to the Great Spirit. Be kind, be valiant, be free, then are the Indians sons of Glory!

In all the wars since, I can tell you what we fought for as Native Veterans. As Chief Orono said over two hundred years ago, should the Revolutionaries lose, the white men would be bound in chains, and we Native people treated like animals. We fought to protect our land, our freedom and our way of life, and yes, we even fought to protect this Country because what happens to the Country, happens to us only much worse.

The military taught us to dehumanize people in order to consider them animals to kill more easily. It has been my life's objective since that realization to humanize my people. I have tried many ways to do that. During my twelve years in the Legislature I sponsored a bill that required all Maine Public Schools to teach Maine Indian History. That bill was enacted into law and now all Maine Public Schools are required to teach about our history as Indian people here in this State. There are a few other accomplishments I realized while serving in the Legislature; among those was the State of the Tribes Address to the Legislature. The Tribal Chiefs were never allowed to address the Legislature since the States creation in 1820. I worked over a year for the Chiefs to be able to address the Legislature, and finally on March 11th 2002, the Chiefs were allowed to address a joint session (House and Senate together) of the Legislature. It was a historical event for Maine and the Chiefs' addresses were carried live on TV and radio and headlined in the newspapers the next day. We were highly visible at least for one day.

Later I put forward to the Legislature a JOINT RESOLUTION IN SUPPORT OF THE UNITED NATIONS DECLARATION ON THE RIGHTS OF INDIGENOUS PEOPLES. It was passed by both Houses unanimously on April 15th 2008. It was the last act of my Legislative Career. Maine was the only State to pass such a resolution. It is one of my key findings that the more the majority culture knows about you as a people and as human beings, the harder it is to eliminate you.

Finally, I want to share my conclusion with you about the lessons I've learned. It can be summed up in one example:

Communication & Education=Understanding (CEU)

I have found that if you can communicate with the people in power and start educating them with your stories and culture, they will begin to understand who you are and that you have families and many of the same needs as they do. This process is not easy and there is mistrust on both sides and rightly so. I maintain that Communication and Education are the keys. I served my time in the State Legislature handicapped without a vote. Tribal Representatives were allowed a seat in the House only, but had no vote. I came to realize that when you don't have all the faculties to make deals with and change hearts and minds on the

Legislative power level, you develop other skills. Your people's survival depends on those verbal skills and other leverage you can use such as other legislators, your friends and allies, and organizations that are supportive. These were all important and what carried us through and kept us alive as Tribal Governments.

Today we are seeing the results of gaining allies and friends. The newly elected Governor Janet Mills, who is the first woman governor in Maine's history won a highly contentious and close race by gaining the support of Tribal allies who insisted that the new governor open up new dialogue with the Tribes and work on ways to move forward together. My hope is that Chief Orono's words will finally come true.

> "… they will return good for good and the law of love runs through their children…"

I believe there is hope.

Donna Loring, 2019

Acknowledgments

The indigenous women interviewed here speak eloquently about the convergence of identity and activism in the twenty-first century. Through their generosity of spirit, expertise, and intellectual prowess, we understand their perspective and gain insight into this topic.

Prior to the taping sessions, I had met only three of these women, thus the majority of them entrusted their words and ideas to me as a stranger. As each spoke to me, I hoped to be involved in some way in the dissemination of their knowledge and praxis. I am grateful for the women who invited me into their homes, or agreed to meet with me as they negotiated my presence between myriad obligations of work and personal life. I travelled to remote spots as needed, relishing the physical and intellectual journeys. I extend my deepest appreciation to everyone who granted me an interview. I thank them all for allowing me to walk with them.

My gratitude extends especially to one individual who requested omission, and Luz Maria for longer conversations, connections, references, and the belief and trust they placed in me. I met Callan Chythlook-Sifsof through my daughter. Callan told me of her experience with the Olympics in Salt Lake City as an Alaska Native. I was teaching a class on indigeneity that semester. I invited her to form part of our class discussion and add her voice to this project.

My friends and colleagues Dr. Anne Fuller and Sharon Williams assisted with editorial work.

Dallas Fawson, initially a graduate student and later invaluable research assistant, played an indispensable role, setting up cameras and recording machines, as well as translating numerous pieces. Dallas was sensitive and discrete in the course of interviewing, and his support throughout the project was unwavering. I am indebted to him in so many ways.

I thank doctoral literature Ph.D. graduates Victor Zabala and Keri Gonzalez for translation work, both of whom brought to English or Spanish, the heart and soul of these women.

Emily Larsen, undergraduate Music major, gave generous time and care to the transcriptions of these voices.

Luise Poulton, recently retired Managing Curator and Head of the Rare Books Department at the J. Willard Marriott Library, The University of Utah, offered generous moral and intellectual support and invaluable guidance. She has developed and curated a fabulous collection. Moreover, she is the finest editor and colleague. This book could never have found its way without her.

I acknowledge the University Research Creative Grants that supported travel and editorial work for many of the transcriptions. Dr. Joanne Yaffe and Mia Lionelli were helpful in managing our new system for grant requests. The Taft-Nicholson Environmental Humanities Center in Montana provided space to edit as a Writing Fellow in 2019. The International Travel Grants from The University of Utah College of Humanities sponsored travel to conferences to present the material. Interim Dean Culver was instrumental in helping me secure grants and release time for writing. In addition, Jake Jensen, Associate Dean of Research provided information on securing external grants and the contact with Writing Fellow Will Smiley.

I am grateful for a research grant extended to me by the UNE Maine Women Writers Collection archives. University of New England Maine Women Writers Collection (UNE-MWWC) Curator Cathleen Miller and Laura Taylor, Metadata Librarian at the Abplanalp Library in Portland, were essential to my success during my week with those collections. Their reading room is an important space for connecting with women writers.

The University of Oregon Special Collections staff assisted me during my visit to their library to view the Winona LaDuke boxes on file.

Thanks to Amy Hague, Mary Biddle and Venice of the Smith College, Sophia Smith Special Collection of Rebecca Adamson papers. The Smith College library funded part of the research trip to their archives. Their library space and instruction on the use of photo equipment made the archives especially accessible.

In Boston, thanks to Lia and Bill Poorvu. At Harvard, the Houghton Special Collections and Tozzer library staff were very helpful. By serendipity, I visited the Peabody Museum, where the exhibit of Native American anthropology is housed, and viewed the pilot series of sound recordings by Native poets that accompanies the walk-through. This playlist introduced me to the voices of Gwen Nell Westerman (Dakota), Tommy Pico (Kumeyaay), Margaret Noodin (Anishinaabe), Eric Gansworth (Onondaga), Tacey M. Atsitty (Diné), Natalie Diaz (Mojave), Trevino L. Brings Plenty (Minneconjou Lakota), dg nanoukokpik (Inupiat-Inuit), from *New Poets of Native Nations* (edited by Heid E. Erdrich, 2018). Many of the themes in these poems reflect the narrative threads of the conversations here on identity, resistance, and social change.

Finally, I love my four children very much and appreciate their love and kindness throughout this project. They are a continuing source of inspiration and encouragement. Oftentimes when the subject matter was overwhelming, they made me smile and prodded me to remember why I do what I do.

1 Introduction

As there has been much said and written about American Indians, with my tribe, the Klamath Indians, included, by the white People, which is guessed at and not facts, I deem it necessary to first tell you, for which please do not criticize me as egotistical. I am a pure, full-blooded Klamath River woman.

Lucy Thompson, To the American Indian

To be an Indian today means to be an inarticulate subject under the plenary power of Congress, presumed by the United States Supreme Court to be governed by Christian motives in its dealings with the ignorant and dependent race. It means to be hungry, sick, and dying while still used for a national political football. Please Oh America, send Christian statesmen to Congress! Demand justice for our Indian today!

Zitkala Sa, Americanize the First American

My name is Rigoberta Menchú. I am twenty-three years old. This is my testimony. I didn't learn it from a book and I didn't learn it alone. I'd like to stress that it's not only my life, it's also the testimony of my people

Rigoberta Menchú, I, Rigoberta Menchú

I don't want anyone at any moment to interpret the story I'm about to tell as something that is only personal. Because I think that my life is related to my people.

> What happened to me could have happened to hundreds of people in my country. I want to make this clear, because I recognize that there have been people who have done much more than I for the people, but who have died or who haven't had the opportunity to be known… I'm proud of the Indian blood in my heart. I am also proud of being the wife of a miner. I would like everyone to be proud of what they are and what they have, of their culture, their language, their music, their way of being and not accept the influences from abroad so much, or try to imitate other people who, ultimately, have given little of worth to our society.
>
> Domitila de Chúngara, *Let Me Speak!*[1]

The conversations in this book begin with an invocation by Lucy Thompson, Che-Na-Wah Weitch-ah-Wah, Yurok Indian. In the preface to her classic 1916 monograph, *To the American Indian,* she opens with a call to all Indigenous Peoples and non-native scholars to beware of false truths or speculation regarding Indians. Our contemporary moment in history recently decried fake news as a constant thematic tweet emanating from the Oval Office. In 1916 and now, taking time to consider sources who are credible is indispensable towards setting, and keeping, the record straight.

Historian Peter Palmquist in his Foreword to *To the American Indian* described Thompson (1856–1932), known as Talth and Che-Na-Wah Weitch-ah-Wah, as "someone who spoke directly from her heart, from her beliefs, from her sad and wise experiences as a member of a tribe whose culture she saw being extinguished before her eyes." Her written commentary was and remains "a valuable contribution to the world's knowledge of a specialized culture of which available descriptions are few." Her writing offered a crucial source of narrative documentation of lifeways, challenges, dichotomies, polemics, and recurring themes that have not dissipated in our times. Che-Na-Wah Weitch-ah-Wah narrates with the express mandate of "telling all in a plain and truthful way, with the least coloring of facts."[2]

She begins: "I am a pure, full-blooded Klamath River woman. In our tongue we call this great river by the name Health-kick-wer-roy, and I wear tattoos on my chin that has been the custom for our women for many generations. I was born at Pee-wan village, and of highest birth or what we term under the highest laws of marriage. I am known by my people as Talth."[3]

Her keen sense of identity is tied to a place and the lineage of her people.

Struck by these reminiscences of a Yurok woman from the early 1900s, I sought out other Native female precursors who might serve as compelling guides to an understanding of current Indigenous voices. Finding sparse examples of century-old handwritten notes, speeches, and manuscripts inspired further inquiry. These forerunners offered a potential narrative structure and thematic organization for publishing contemporary Indigenous women's voices, the interviews privileged in this manuscript. The path on which intrepid Indigenous women describe themselves, and their commitment to the protection and revitalization of a colonized, marginalized cultural worldview began to materialize.

Talth was committed to salvaging the scant traces of a pre-conquest heritage from post-colonization devastation. Although she was not alone, she was one of only a few native women who wrote in the early 1900s in their effort to bridge worlds that had collided.

Zitkala Sa, Gertrude Bonnin (1876–1938), Sioux South Dakota native, was another early activist who motivated my work here. Her obituary read "American Indians' … staunchest friend and most diligent worker in their behalf." Acclaimed by *The New York Times* as "a champion of her race," Zitkala Sa wrote of Native identity in the first decades of the twentieth century.[4] With caustic precision, she explicitly tackled "America's Indian Problem," the title of one of her essays.

Zitkala Sa's advocacy, beyond initially publishing the legends and short stories of her people in the *Atlantic Monthly*, *Harpers*, and educational publications by *Ginn & Co.*, entailed employment as a clerk in the Indian Service, subsequent to teaching in the Indian boarding schools. Her experiences within these positions sparked her activism. She lobbied the United States Congress about the dire circumstances of poverty and illiteracy of Native Americans. She published detailed reports about the devastating life on American reservations, based on over 12,000 miles covered at her own expense by car in 1926. Her crusading took the form of direct action based on firsthand collaboration on the reservations with Indian Service employees. As founder and President of the National Council of American Indians and Secretary of the Society of American Indians she wrote letters to legislators and State Supreme Court justices and gave speeches before federations of women's clubs.

Zitkala-Sa was an outspoken advocate whose untiring efforts strove to illuminate and "remedy by way of congressional bills" the inequities and dire conditions faced by Indigenous populations in the United States. In a letter dated April 1932, she solicited funds for "salvaging remnants of its tribes, and thereby, as liaison agent…assist America's reclamation of her own aborigines, before it is too late." In *Americanize the First American: A Plan of Regeneration*, her inquiry turned to a meticulous comparison of the disparities between abundant white material privilege in a small western town versus the gross absence of wealth on the Pine Ridge reservation. In a different report to the Office of Indian Rights

Associations, the title of her audacious research accounting is *An Orgy of Graft and Exploitation of Indian Probate Situation*. She spared few words in seeking due process of the law, decrying the "poor conditions in Native American Schools" based on her observations of the evident privation on reservations from 1925 to 1928. She wrote, "The Indian race is starving—not only physically but mentally and morally." Denouncing the actual workers in the Indian service as "Indian haters," her writings reflect the same themes and conflicts brokered by the contemporary changemakers here.[5]

Moved by these courageous advocates from early twentieth century North America, my research veered to the Southern and Central Latin American regions, where printed documentation of and/or by Indigenous women is almost nonexistent. The most prominent examples from the region are testimonials of/by Indigenous women in Latin America from the 1970s to 1980s. Two quintessential voices were Aymara Bolivian Domitila Barrios de Chúngara and Nobel Peace Prize winner Rigoberta Menchú. Their ground-breaking oral narratives of identity formation and social consciousness honed direct action utilizing the eclectic genre of *testimonio*—a complex form of post-colonial life writing about oppression and dispossession. In the case of the first work, *Let me Speak! Testimony of Domitila, a Woman of the Bolivian Mines*, exposed the exploitation and quashing of basic rights of an Indigenous Bolivian mine worker. The latter work, *I, Rigoberta Menchú, An Indian Woman in Guatemala* (1983) was a comparable catalyst through a first-hand account of the genocide committed against Indigenous Peoples during the Guatemalan Civil War (1960–1996) and the conditions of the Guatemalan Indigenous People in the twentieth century.

These two texts, edited and compiled by non-Native academic anthropologists and sociologists, brought, in print, the first quasi-autoethnographic examples by Indigenous women to global audiences. John Beverley noted that the "bourgeoise public sphere" to which these women at that time had no access for written intervention was precisely the site of contestation where they sought to bear witness to their "very conditions of subalternity."[6]

Testimonio graphically represented their political, social, economic, and psychological subjugation in their own words. The women described consciousness raising, identity formation, Indigenous lifeways and practices, the circumstances of their violent oppression, and self-described political awakening. Central to the significance of *testimonio* genre lay its' manifest urgency to tell and denounce the reality of living as an Indigenous *campesina*, as a miner, or as a laborer in Bolivia or Guatemala specifically. Clear connections to First People's plight, with its correlative oppression, in other countries could be drawn. Endemic to the highly controversial *testimonio* of the mid-to-late twentieth century, Menchú and Barrios de Chúngara became activists in the mere telling, describing, denouncing, publicizing, and, in some instances, engaging in political work, to change global mindsets about the killings, exploitation, and abuse of their people.

Testimonio was a unique rhetorical form of activism, resistant to formal definition, and "at the crossroads of all the discourses of institutional battles in recent years," as Gugelberger stated at the height of the polemic around the genre.[7] Döring categorizes it "a threshold genre" that "traces and crosses boundaries between fact and fiction, memory and history, selves and others, homes and exile—sometimes drawing these distinctions but more often blurring them"—allowing for self-creation in the interview setting and subsequent international publication.[8] The salient characteristics of *testimonio* made it an ideal type of life-writing that exposed and condemned dire conditions, even atrocities, to which Native women were subjected. Menchú's book begins, "The important thing is that what has happened to me has happened to many other people too; my story is the story of all poor Guatemalans. My personal experience is the reality of a whole people."[9] The narrator, Indigenous Woman, was generally illiterate, poor, and marginalized and would not have found outlet for the depiction of injustice facing herself as individual, and also as a member of her people. Still, the value of *testimonio*, this direct narration, supplanted her academic interlocuter.

I refer back to this embryonic, post-colonial life-writing because I consider it seminal for contextualizing the twenty-first-century self-representations by Indigenous women from around the globe. Today they deploy directly into global communications networks and can circumvent the complicated mediation by a learned interviewer that had become so common to *testimonio*. My explicit goal in this book is to move past the controversy of *testimonio* to bring this series of interviews with a wide spectrum of Native women into a comparative framework, as similar and divergent. Further, this book corroborates the capacity of these women to be shapers of dialogue in their own right.

However, it is imperative to acknowledge the problematic aspects of *testimonio* genre, specifically that mediation of the Indigenous subject's voice and authorial control maintained by the non-Indigenous anthropologist author. The mediation replicated aspects of the colonization of subjectivity, discourse, and narrative, which may be seen to incur a form of violence in speaking for the other. Gayatri Spivak asked—"Can the Subaltern Speak?"[10] The contested answer would be a resounding no, at least within the parameters of testimonial or other life-writing narrative forms within mediation. My objective is, in part, to conduct a meta-analysis of this type of collaboration and problematizing of subjectivity, both of which remain precarious within the framework of the Indigenous. In conversation with many of the interviewees, we sifted through that polemic to examine our endeavor. It is in the words and perspective of these activists that we confront ourselves against their views of Indigenous activism and reality. Their responses illustrate the direct impact of lack of access to institutional accountability and hence, justice for their communities. Given that these women wield the power of their own voice and presence on social media and other communication outlets, this book is a mode of bringing diverse speakers together into one space for the reader to compare.

Indigenous women utilize, with great skill, social media channels like Twitter, Instagram, Facebook, and YouTube for the dissemination of their resistance work and identity. They contribute to, and mobilize, social media and news sources with notable presence on global data platforms. We need only examine the work of Daniella Zalcman photojournalist on Instagram and in hard copy books. Callan Chythlook-Sifsof (US Olympian snowboarder) posted on Instagram allegations of sexual harassment, and opposition to oil development in Bristol Bay Alaska. Singer Sara Curruchich streams regularly on Instagram (@saracurruchich), and posts live podcasts. Liliana Hernandez frequently decries injustice on Facebook. Davina Dah Yi'itihi, who is running for Utah State House of Representatives in District 69 (2022) utilizes Facebook, Instagram, and a campaign website. Honorable Donna Loring leads a weekly radio talk show.

I make no pretense of crafting a uniform narrative with me as the interlocutor of the conversation. Rather, as non-native editor I have privileged the discussion of content delving into identity, feminism, and resistance work, in relation to the historical global context of Native woman as activist in the twenty-first century. I interviewed individuals known for change work in diverse non-political professions, of Indigenous descent and upbringing, high levels of educational attainment, and hailing from distinct geographies in order to glean theoretical and practical points of convergence and divergence for use in the classroom. A broader audience of native and non-native readers may well be inspired by this generation of Indigenous women who reflect potential and resolve.

From the original canon of testimonial narratives several themes emerge beyond the dire rebukes and exposure of malfeasance, brutality, and genocide that apply here. Domitila, the forgotten activist, consecrates *Let Me Speak!* to "reach the poorest people, who don't have any money, but need orientation, some example that can serve them in their future life. To the poor who have nothing else."[11] She wrote knowing that words themselves can nourish and guide even the most impoverished individuals. Elizabeth Cook-Lynn, Professor Emerita of

English and Native American Studies, points out, "Writing is an essential act of survival for contemporary American Indians."[12] An act of survival and self-affirmation for themselves and for their communities.

In the interviews, the desire to speak out and act for posterity is frequently repeated. Invoking the resilience of their ancestors and, in particular, hailing mothers and grandmothers, the remonstration rekindles and burns. There is a commitment to tell a story for descendants, for those afraid to speak, or for those unable to act. Two interviewees, in an emotional recounting of their past experiences of discrimination and professional engagement, dedicated their words and conversations to the future survival of their People, their sons, daughters, and the multitudinous victims of rape, pillaging, plunder, and exploitation. Their willingness to speak about very traumatic events so as to give voice to silenced narratives are poignant reminders of the courage needed to expose the complicity and cover-up by abusers of power and position.

Diné Davina Dah Yi'itihi Smith (Spotted Elk at the time of interview) relayed her abuse in the boarding school system. She has begun to speak about it so others might do so as well and find a seat in what she calls the "restorative circle."

> I kept quiet all these years since my youth. With the knowledge I have now, I wish I would've opened up a long time ago. I've had the experience others endured, and I didn't say anything. Now that I'm able to open up, I know, first and foremost, it wasn't my fault. I know that, but when I hear other women, say "Oh…let's not talk about that, I don't want to hear that." In fact, I feel strongly we must talk about it. Please. I see that holding in what I have for so long, does something to you. For me to release it was a feeling of … [strong exhale].[13]

Smith clings to her identity as a Navajo woman and her legacy stemming from the knowledge imparted by her activist grandmother Katherine Smith (featured in the documentary *Broken Rainbow*),[14] that grounds and fortifies her. Her strength is rooted in language, culture, place, and understanding of herself in the continuum of Native ancestors and future progeny. From this, she speaks out.

> Whenever I'm not balanced in the city, I can always go back home and find rejuvenation there. I know that now. I can connect with my mother who is a Navajo language teacher. If the language that I miss can't come out of my mouth, I can talk to my parents. It gives me strength. I can go anywhere in the world and get up before the dawn and greet the holy people to the east. That knowledge and awareness gives me energy, determination, and balance. I take that legacy to

> heart, in how I carry myself wherever I go; How I speak; How I listen. Also, as a mother, I have to carry myself in a certain way, because one day my daughter will be the same. My son will have a wife, and will have to know how to treat her with respect.[15]

Maya lawyer Liliana Hernandez positions her feminism in the context of the Indigenous movement of the twenty-first century—as a role model and loudspeaker for her community.

> I am an Indigenous woman and a lawyer, and the first woman to graduate from a university in both my maternal and paternal family. That makes me feel very honored, and it is a greater duty to use the profession that I studied in service of my community and the Indigenous people of Guatemala.
>
> I fight for justice, for the collective rights of the Indigenous people. With my testimony of life and struggle, other women feel motivated and inspired to move forward, to change those traditional gender roles which state that they should only be at home making food and taking care of children. I do that as well, but I also have a profession. I project myself onto my community and on all of the Guatemalan population in the struggle for rights.
>
> I am a woman of struggle. A socially-committed lawyer, which means a lawyer that is not simply in their office waiting for clients, but one that fights for the fulfillment of the rights of Indigenous women and Indigenous communities, especially in the defense of natural resources.[16]

Black activist Viola Davis at the US Woman's March in 2018 verbalized an analogous sentiment regarding the motivation to, and rewards of, raising one's voice, particularly for those who can't: "The women who are faceless. The women who don't have the money and don't have the constitution and who don't have the confidence and who don't have the images in our media that gives them a sense of self-worth enough to break their silence that is rooted in the shame of assault and rooted in the stigma of assault".[17]

Many reasons inhibit the oppressed from speaking out. Fear of violent retribution for public protest or justified skepticism about a privileged terminology that seems to only speak for the colonizer can hinder individuals from donning the highly-charged label of "activist" or "feminist." Various of these interviewees reject the labels of Western feminist or activist only to reframe and ground the categorization in their own theory of Indigenous feminist activism, or *feminismo comunitario* [community (tribal nation-based) feminism]—counter-hegemonic feminism.

Social anthropologist Aura Cumes rejects entirely the label of feminism and its epistemological premise.

> I am not a feminist. Neither a community-descended [from the ethno linguistic community] feminist, nor a decolonial feminist, in spite of the fact that I am in all of these groups. I am a part of GLEFAS (Latin American Group of Studies, Training and Feminist Action). They know that I am not a feminist. I support the struggle for decolonization and the anti-patriarchal struggles. However, I do not identify as a feminist because I do not believe that what I do only stems, and can be understood, from the perspective of feminism.
>
> Feminism is only a part of what I do, and when feminism arrogantly places itself in a position of saying "until we came along, women had not opened their eyes," it immediately co-opts the struggle. I do not want to be co-opted by anyone. The epistemologies that I am trying to vindicate in this moment do not come from feminism. I respect feminism and I have learned from it, but I do not identify as a feminist. The necessary critique that I make of the version of feminism that has arrived here in Guatemala is that the history of women does not begin in Europe or the United States.
>
> Here, the history of women and of their struggles always begins when the lives of women are being threatened. That premise permits us to observe and think about the past, the struggles of women in the colonial era, and even earlier. However, in the colonial era and during the dictatorship, in the era of genocide, an important women's struggle emerges. If we think ignorantly that until feminism in the 1980s came along women had never opened their eyes, it closes our mind to the broader endeavors of resistance by women. For that reason, I do not accept it.
>
> My dialogue with the past is a premise that allows me to think that this dialogue can take place anywhere. I do not consider myself a feminist, because that implies subordinating myself epistemologically to feminism, which is something I reject.[18]

Lucia Xiloj, a Maya lawyer, works tirelessly in defense of the Indigenous women raped during the Guatemalan Civil War. She pushes back on definitions of feminism that obfuscate Indigeneity and its struggles.

> I do not identify as a feminist. I work towards women's rights, and the feminism that is practiced in Guatemala still has not managed to understand that Indigenous women have a distinct perception and merit freedom as they understand feminist causes. Feminism offers a form of strengthening women that clashes with the process we Indigenous women are involved in to vindicate ourselves and to overcome our historical subordination. Sometimes feminism arrives

> suddenly and forcefully, and for that reason Indigenous women do not connect with it.[19]

For some, feminism *is* activism and derives from their mothers' example of resistance. Callan Chythlook-Sifsof explains:

> My feminism comes from my mom. When I was at an early age, she was really a fighter, an activist, a feminist, though not self-identified as such. She has always been an activist, not about only one issue, rather about women's issues, Indigenous [Yupik] issues and so forth. In a world where there are many smart people, coming from the village, she wanted to learn. You and I were talking about how white people speak for native people. In the era when I was growing up, there was a lot of white influence coming in, MTV and cable starting up—that socio-cultural colonial imperialism of the modern era, which took place here [lower continent] a while ago, it began there [Alaska] in my youth. So, we were a pure culture that began to have negative things starting to happen and seep in.[20]

Liliana Hernandez seeks justice for Indigenous Peoples by advocating for awareness vis-a-vis the threats to Indigenous women and their People.

> I have had the opportunity to join struggles for the defense of rivers and other water sources, and for the defense and the recovery of lands. This gives me the certainty that we are contributing to the eradication of many inequalities—not only of an ethnic origin, but economic inequalities as well, because when a woman is economically independent, she can also be free to better face the violence that exists against women. She can overcome and survive situations of violence. If a woman has the possibilities and opportunities as well as the economic means to move forward, it can contribute to reduce the inequality gaps facing women.
>
> I live in Guatemala, a country that is racist, discriminatory, patriarchal, and misogynistic, and in that context, I fight by means of my profession as a lawyer. As an activist, I participate in social collectives and in other spaces, like organizations or spaces of analysis. This means often our actions of resistance are not simply in accompanying a group of people in a legal sense, but rather in equipping these struggles with the understanding about rights and protest, and through social networks, offering messages of support to the demands of the population, not only of the Indigenous people. We also support the citizens that, in this Guatemalan context, fight against the impunity and corruption of this nation in which we, the Indigenous people are not included, and where women also have no place.
>
> In support of the inclusion of Indigenous women, I have participated in endeavors, initiated by the government and from social organizations, specifically

> the *Defensoría de la Mujer Indígena* (Advocacy for Indigenous Women), an institution which was created as a product of the peace treaties, with the intention on the part of several women that it would be for Indigenous women.
>
> However, within the structure of a racist nation, this institution has also faced discrimination. There is structural discrimination on the part of the nation towards these smaller opportunities to assist Indigenous women. The entire struggle, and these recent experiences reaffirms our commitment that we must do more work and leave a legacy of life for other generations to transform our situation.[21]

Juana Batzibal Tujal, a United Nations human rights defender who has worked with NGOs in Mexico and Central America links feminism inseparably to activism and ethnicity.

> We, as Indigenous women, sometimes do not respect our own vision for the feminist movement. We always consider that the feminists must work for Maya women or other Indigenous women everywhere. The politicians are stuck in a mentality that we are juvenile, or incapable of proposing action or concrete plans. We must make everyone understand there is another way to envision contestation and change, a different way to understand life, and that we can chime in and add our energy and strength in order to change patriarchal thought that has been enshrouded within the Guatemalan State.[22]

One message regarding feminism these women bring to the fore is that one need not identify as "feminist" in order to do feminist work. First People's women activists redefine how people understand feminism itself, using their lives and their work as example. Many voices play a unique part in altering the paradigms, discourse, and rhetoric of the subjugation of Indigenous women and their nations.

Tara Houska,[23] of Honor the Earth organization, reflects, "It's not as hard as you think it is to be engaged...there are lots of different roles to play. It takes not just one angle—it takes everything, all together, to make a change."

Activism

Fall 2017 saw a flux in overt criminalization and violent reactions by authorities to social protest by Indigenous Peoples in the Americas. Efforts towards the criminalization of civic protest increased around the globe. On October 30, 2017 an email from a LASA-ERIP listserv posted by a member of the preeminent association of professionals working on Latin American studies copied an unnerving death threat targeted at the lives of specific Indigenous people, women and men, for their professional and resistance work. Examining the list of individuals named, and their corresponding professions, it is disturbing to see spokespeople, candidates for the national legislature, journalists, environmental scientists, and others silenced in their endeavors to (1) make public the destruction of their lands, and the unsustainable extraction of natural resources, and (2) halt the ongoing erasure of cultural heritage and annihilation of their people.[24]

Every day, still, another Indigenous person, many women included, is targeted outright. A *Cultural Survival Quarterly* headline reads, "Patricia Gualinga Montalvo, Indigenous Kichwa leader and lifelong defender of the Amazon rainforest in her community of Sarayaku, Ecuador, received death threats and her home was attacked in Puyo, Ecuador, on January 5, 2018."[25] A *Global Witness* report states that "227 land and environmental activists were murdered in 2020 for defending their land and the planet. That constitutes the highest number ever recorded for a second consecutive year."[26] There were, and continue to be in 2022, activists following orthodox scripts, asserting legally-sanctioned dissent, or taking on leadership positions, who find themselves receiving threats for that direct action.

Others, however, advocate another form of protest and resistance that assumes a different guise. This other expression of activism is what is captured in these interviews. The intimidation of legally-sanctioned dissenters spurred this inquiry into how Indigenous women were speaking about activism and how, if at all, it might still be viable. Social protesters, protecting their lands, like Standing Rock, were targeted in violent ways. Because of its actions against this particular resistance, the United States, paragon of democracy, ticked down several notches from its rank as a champion of human rights and freedom of speech in indices produced by NGOs such as Transparency International.[27] Nations in the Latin American region with similarly inscribed guaranteed rights in their constitutions enacted egregious breaches of civil and human rights, specifically against Indigenous Peoples. In 2017 the *World Press Freedom Index*, published by Reporters Without Borders, and *Freedom in the World* report on global human rights violations, repression, and erosion of the rule of law wrote alarmingly about the worldwide increase of detentions and murder of civilians, in what they called a "current crisis of democracy." Indigenous activists ranked highest on the death toll.[28]

The effect of this delegitimizing of protest has been one of redefining activism. Activism in its current context, bearing real-time consequences, extends beyond conventional definitions. The mounting omnipresence of social media and communication networks has been transforming the configuration, articulation, and dissemination as much as the democratization of activism as advocating energetic direct action and the commensurate twenty-first century social protest movements.

Mississauga Nishnaabeg Leanne Betasamosake Simpson in a 2016 speech to the *American Studies Association* traced the roots of "new solidarity actions—*instances of acting*" [my emphasis]—in response precisely to the ongoing neutralization of resistance strategies. State-sanctioned methods of dissension face criminalization and intimidation requiring alternative modes of protest. There are three aspects Simpson highlighted: (1) generative refusal, (2) culturally-affirmative recognition, and (3) reciprocity.

She explained how Mohawk Audra Simpson's powerful "re-embedding of belonging" comes to life through collective Indigenous intelligence, groundbreaking interventions, and synergies of "intelligence excellence." This means drawing on the collective knowledge base of millenary Indigenous Peoples to craft a *productive* place of refusal. Grounding oneself in the Indigenous knowledge of centuries-old practices and epistemologies seeks generative processes rather than exploitation or destruction. "Colonial recognition" is rejected as the starting point. Instead, one appeals to a politics of "generative refusal," that is propagative and productive, allowing for "instances of acting as people who belong to specific nations." Taken together with Glen Coulthard's *Red Skin, White Mask*, Betasamosake Simpson reclaims the definition of recognition central to Native cultural thought: "it is about presence, about profound listening and about recognizing and affirming the light in each other, as a mechanism for nurturing and strengthening internal relationships to our Nishnaabeg worlds." She pinpoints the centrality of reciprocity, reflecting and mirroring back as self-identity—seeing oneself and oneself as told by another.[29]

The concept of reciprocity cardinal to many Native worldviews prompted me to publish as much of the direct transcription of these interviews as possible. These contemporary conversations "cognitively reverse the violence of dispossession," of silencing, and of erasure of Indigenous woman.[30] Seeing/witnessing, listening/hearing and accepting/giving printed form to their complete stories for others to fully encounter makes space for this generative reversal and empowerment.

Repeatedly, for these interviewees, activism is aligned with specific Indigenous cultural heritage—Native culture as synonymous with resistance. A former Honor the Earth staff member says: "Activism is action you commit yourself to. For me, activism and activists are the folks that are recognizing the past given to them, carved and forged by the people who came before us. We are doing this work for the people who come after us…I like to say I am a human being, who does the work that needs to be done for future generations. I characterize my work as a facet of my indigeneity."[31] Betasamosake Simpson speaking with Naomi Klein, clarified this point: "this isn't a cause for me—this is my life."[32] Cristina Marin, Mapuche from Northern Argentina, reinforces both women: "activism is a constant in our lives. It is part of our daily struggle and our resistance."[33] Long-time iconic Chippewa environmental activist Winona LaDuke, while a Harvard undergrad, said, "My work is my life. Uranium and coal mining are the two most crucial issues Indians have to deal with. Because when you talk about repression, you talk about genocide, you talk about sterilization of Indian women, it all ties back to these resources. They wouldn't be doing this to us otherwise."[34]

As more native women achieve higher levels of education, and operate in public spaces previously denied to Indigenous People and more so to Indigenous women, the nature of resistance is changing. At its core, it is a solidarity movement shared by many. Sara Curruchich, international singer performer, says, "I see music, my form of engagement in the realm of art, as a very powerful tool. Through music you can share messages, make an impact, and raise consciousness. It can bring awareness."[35] A DAPL protest organizer points out, "There are so many ways people are resisting that do not look like what our elders did, or resemble what our adversaries think that it should be, according to their preconceived notions; like setting things on fire or looting. Many of us are here resisting in new ways."[36] These approaches fit well into a currently emerging counter-hegemonic anti-globalization discourse that Hans Fernandez Benitez calls a "renovated testimonial episteme which continues to promote international solidarity and consciousness of human rights."[37]

No matter how monumental or trivial a bleep on the barometer of change, each adds another ancestral kernel of a non-GMO maize to the mound needed to prepare tortillas or bread and nourish life.[38] Choctaw Ethnobotanist, Native American scholar, Franci Taylor offered this analogy: "one molecule in a bottle at a time is where we start and continue, but slowly the bottle is filled."[39]

One by one, the kernels are collectively stockpiled. In a review of Pamela Yates' documentary film *500 Years*, premiering at the 2017 Sundance Film Festival, the Los Angeles Times wrote, "resistance is rarely useless."[40] Expert witness and social anthropologist, Irma Velásquez Nimatuj, is featured in the film as one of the many women who brought some justice to the Guatemalan Indigenous women victims of the Rios Montt reign of rape and genocide.[41] IMDb distributor describes the film as portraying the "mounting resistance played out in Guatemala's recent history through the actions and perspectives of the majority Indigenous Mayan population, who now stand poised to *reimagine* their society."[42]

Social Anthropology, also called Activist Anthropology, emerged in the late 1990s to bridge the gap between praxis and academia. It is a field that found institutional support in the late 1990s, and informed the ten-year collection of *peritajes* (specialist/expert court reports), the gathering of ethnographic testimony about rape and murders in Guatemala. The expert witness role was protagonized by Maya scholars and lawyers (some interviewed here) and consequently struck deep painful chords. Described in first-person, their activism entails collaborative endeavors with the victim/plaintiffs in the judicial courts in order to restore some compassion, humaneness and justice into a dehumanizing legal practice.

As I listened to the interviewees, their tack steered me onto a course of engendered and ethnicized definitions of activism. A kind of estuary of intersecting identities formed. The imperative to acknowledge heterogeneous *roots* and *enactments* of social justice engagement by Indigenous women rose to the surface. Moreover, they queried the pernicious consequences of the overlay of a colonized mindset that predicates a white Western feminism or occidental model of development on Indigenous women's identity, activism, and/or sense of self.

This framework pointed to an alternative model of collaborative, restorative, and regenerative activism. The common terrain grounding these interviews is the human capacity for collaboration in resistance work: transformation takes place through cooperation and synergy—shared platforms, shared intelligence, and collective agendas aspiring to reach a global scale. Academics, in tandem with non-professional women, transgress boundaries of gender, ethnicity, race, culture, economics, and education in order to propose a new system. The words of the so-called non-professional bring to life the gendered dynamics of globalization and mobilization, while underscoring the local instances of resistance. In sum, the collaborative model heralds potential points of entry for creating a more equitable future and addressing systemic reform.

Other definitions of activism seeped into my overview of the topic. I borrowed from Eve Ensler, author of *Vagina Monologues*, who indirectly elucidated a generalized framework: "An activist is someone who cannot help but fight for something. That person is not usually motivated by a need for power or money or fame, but in fact, is driven slightly mad by some injustice, some cruelty, some unfairness, so much so that he or she is compelled by some internal moral engine to act to make it better."[43]

Winona LaDuke, former vice-presidential candidate, in several TED Talks, described activism in relation to precepts of the Indigenous ethical code and value system embodied in "*Minobimaatisiiwin*—the good life:" the choice to walk on either of two paths for humanity. One is the scorched earth (extreme extraction, addiction to fossil-fuels, homogenized monoculture); the other an untrodden Green (renewable, sustainable, vitamin-rich, poverty-reducing). For LaDuke, preserving cultural patrimony and agrobiodiversity incarnates activism. Going from "teepee to Tesla" is a political act for the common good of humans, animal, and all of nature. She lays out the urgency and cognitive logic of enshrining and honoring the rights of the Earth by protecting rice, because "if the rice dies, we die."[44] Activism is based on critical thinking that questions paradigms produced by colonial settler white supremacy—primarily the premise of superiority of white management of natural resources over the lifeways of Native people who have inhabited their lands for millennia.

From another angle, Indigenous economist and activist of Swedish, Cherokee, and Lumbee grandparents, Rebecca Adamson, founded an NGO called First Peoples Worldwide and another called the First Nations Development Institute. In a video on *Makers*, she traces the evolution of her own process of becoming conscious of the material poverty and psychological colonization of Native people in the United States. Her global activism for Indigenous People began at a young age in grassroots activities on reservations, visiting Indian schools and fighting to establish the Indian school reformation crusade. Adamson calls it a civil rights' movement for Indian people. Legislation protecting the Natives' right to self-determination of any and all governmental services and management of their resources is key.[45] Looking at activism through the collective lens of culture and self-articulated community needs, she continues to promote macro and micro socio-economic structural change with consultation.

The importance (and danger) of the work and words of Adamson and others is reflected by the author of the preface to this book. Penobscot Elder Donna Loring, in her book, *In the Shadow of the Eagle*, wrote of her experience working for change at the Maine State Legislature as a non-voting tribal representative: "We are like a tightrope walker who is doing a balancing act between two worlds with a fiery pit below. If we make it across, we will have a bright and productive future as tribes; if we fall, we will burst into flames and cease to exist."[46]

Finally, though not exhaustive in our redaction of Indigenous women's views on activism, Kichwa Nina Pacari, former Ecuadorian Minister of External Relations, shifts the dynamic from what her career as government official dictated to a silent revolution of edification of the *mestizo* and white people. She states, [with] "juridical recognition of Indigenous Peoples [in Ecuador] in place, it is now time to put those legal rights into practice." Instruction, education, and enlightenment of the non-Indigenous by way of explanation and transmittal of Indigenous values, epistemology, and cosmovision must occur. Her path of activism along the "spinal vertebrate of America" involves educating and conversing. Just as her millenary ancestors walked, she advocates that "Indigenous Knowledge is critical to human organic survival."[47]

A 1992 issue of *Cultural Survival Quarterly*, a publication which positions in center stage Indigenous women's activism, addressed what is abundantly clear: "In native communities of Canada and the United States, women are central to traditional ways of life, to indigenous economic power, and to the resistance of so many native peoples to large-scale development projects and other abuses of power."[48]

Themes

The interviews in this book follow several thematic threads, reflecting the drive to speak out on activism and identity: (1) a sense of place based on where one is born that grounds and fortifies identity and existence; (2) an awareness of the dynamics of intersectionality: gender, ethnicity, race, and cultural identity for a native woman today; (3) a refusal to adopt an identity imposed by the colonizer, and distancing of self from the label of "feminist"; (4) acknowledgement of the implications of identity on praxis as multi-valanced; (5) an affirmation of resistance as innate to culture; and (6) recognition of the healing power of words in conversation.

Claims to Indigenous identity are often parallel, yet manifest idiosyncrasy of place and circumstance for each interviewee. *En masse*, as they self-identify, they reject the systemic, sexist dysfunction and normalization of racism and discrimination in any form. Taken together, the themes demarcate a central focus of what it means to be an Indigenous woman today. They also specifically highlight the greatest challenges faced by Native People and debunk the misnomer of "the Indian Problem." Further they attest to colonialism and anti-Indigenous racism as underlying causes for violence against women and ongoing economic, environmental, social, and political oppression.

The content echoes Annie Dodge Wauneka's biography *I'll Go and Do More*, where she references a speech on the Observance of International Women's Year in 1975. As a member of the National Commission, Wauneka (1910–1997) outlined issues that Indian women saw as critical at that time: "protection of Indian lands as a means of maintaining the language, spirit, emotional ties, and tribal values of each group: protection of the land's resources; strengthening of tribal government; reaffirmation of the tribal-federal relationship; and the ability of the tribal government to negotiate for federal funds and use them for effective programs and services." None are tackled solely for the benefit of Indigenous women. Wauneka stresses the intricate correlative relationship between tribal community objectives and positive outcomes for Native women.[49]

At the forefront is the imperative to humanize Indigenous People, to provide a megaphone to their worldview, in order to transform the social imaginary and the material circumstances under which they live. The narratives here express the heartrending, personal impact of social injustice on the speakers' lives—how identity is affected by a pervasive unequal treatment simply because one dons Indigenous garb, an identity that is determined by continual generational denial of access to health, food, employment, and educational resources. These narratives depict identity as it is shaped by ubiquitous colonizers' cultural stereotypes and imagery that is derogatory and racist. They speak to the internalization of discrimination, the colonization of the mind by means of ongoing violent oppression. They describe the microaggressions rampant in quotidian existence.[50] Similarly, they denounce macroaggressions reinforced by socio-economic and political material relations and infrastructure.

In contrast to, and rebuttal of, those oppressive structural barriers to healthy existence and identity formation, these women draw on the resilience of their ancestors to reclaim an identity that is focused, imbued, and resounding with their cultural principles and tenets. Whether she is educated, living off reservation, or in urban dwellings, as Wauneka wrote, "Yet she is an Indian. Her belief is within her. Her heritage is within her.... She... will always remain an Indian."[51] Hence there is an insistence on the normalization of a world view and approach to living, based on Indigenous culture that values growth and grounding in Indigenous values. Wauneka cites Changing Woman, who balances traditional and modern beliefs, with cooperation between people.[52] LaDuke reinforces this concept: "we bring seeds [literally] to the table, in order to sprout diversity, equality, and sustainable self-sufficiency for all."[53]

Others have highlighted themes from their specific locus of enunciation. Grace Ouellette, in giving background and a framework of theory and praxis to the Canadian Aboriginal Women's movement, outlines the main issues that concern them: "their home environments, land dispossession and displacement, loss of traditional economies and customs, the rights to self-determination and self-government, and other societal problems affecting their communities as whole than with male domination." Her *The Fourth World: An Indigenous Perspective on Feminism and Aboriginal Women's Activism*, serves as a reader on the specificity of Aboriginal Canadian women's multi-oppression. Ouellette's approach posits the primary assumption that any study cannot be representative of all Aboriginal women. She severs and stamps out the notion of "aboriginal women as *objects* of research," and, instead, explores misrepresentation, misinterpretation, and factors impacting colonized status, subverting the "treatment [of Aboriginal women] as static remnants of the fur trade," honoring and privileging Indigenous woman's optics through cross-cultural, feminist, legal, political and socio-economic lenses.[54]

Mary Hawkesworth's *Globalization and Feminist Activism* stands out in a similar regard. The goal, for Hawkesworth, is to engender globalization and, concomitantly, ethnicize feminist activism. She identifies the centrality of reclaiming human rights in discourse. Taken further, the implementation of a human rights framework is indispensable to the common good, the ultimate objective of feminist global activists. Quoting Temma Kaplan about the Good for which activists engage, her emphasis is on the fulfillment of "life in which safe housing, proper health, food, education, air and water [are] assured." In addition, Hawkesworth frames feminism "across a variety of intellectual, historical, political, geographic, and temporal" paths. Consequently, feminism spans "repudiation to eschewing labels, to adhering to strategic insights, satisfying practical gender interests, International feminist mobilizations," and more.[55] *Globalization and Feminist Activism* in its girth and scope helps bring cohesion to the multitudinous threads of narrated identities relayed in these interviews.

The edited volume *Global Feminism: Transnational Women's Activism, Organizing, and Human Rights* begins by defining feminism as the "broad goal of challenging and changing gender relations that subordinate women to men and that thereby differentially advantage some women and men relative to others." The book examines the intersectionality of global feminism and transnational activism to advance the notion of heterogeneous feminist activism. Pointing to a variety of feminisms, the essays highlight the shift occurring from exclusively local foci to "thinking and acting within a transnational, planetary/human-oriented theater to effectuate change in a campaign for recognition of women's full personhood, transcending borders physical, geographical, political, socio-economic, colonial in all senses."[56]

The turn of the twenty-first century marked a pivotal point in the theorization of intersectionality of transglobal social movements, identity politics, gender studies, and alternative knowledge production, such as the work of Naples & Desai on transnational feminisms.[57] Publications examine the recent manifestations of resistance work as recounted in ethnographic discourse, solidarity activism, engendered social justice activism in Latin America and Caribbean, transborder missing and murdered Native women, Native women's activism in urban communities, and environmental activism, to cite only a few of the flourishing fields of research.[58]

A newer book on Indigenous/Aboriginal/Native women's activism delves into their role in "leadership, creating community accountable approaches, and Indigenous feminist analyses of violence" regarding the escalating number of disappeared Native women.[59] Missing women in Canada, Mexico, and parts of the United States is a topic only recently being investigated.[60]

Indigenous women's activism in Chiapas and Oaxaca has consistently received considerable attention since the 1990s uprisings. An updated edition of *Dissident Women* is one of the go-to books on militancy and activism by women in that region.

Cultural Survival Inc and its' respective *Quarterly* have prioritized activities and publication of articles about global Native people's rights, activism, and cultures.[61] The organization advocates for their rights and supports Indigenous self-determination, cultures, and political resilience. On the cover and in the body of nearly every issue stand women—leading indigenous protest and resisting settler colonialism and environmental extraction projects.

Indigenous Activism Profiles of Native Women in Contemporary America most closely resembles my project. It offers a collection of essays about eighteen Native American women activists and provides a history of women's advocacy from colonization onward, with biographical information in each chapter about these North American women activists. The introduction establishes and acknowledges women's role as activists. It also presents a wide selection of personalities and professional backgrounds, although without the comparative stroke of Latin American Indigenous women.

Maylei Blackwell, prominent scholar of Indigenous studies, has charted transborder activism for groups with shared goals as they navigate geographies of difference. Her focus is on the activism shared across borderlands. In comparison to Blackwell's work, I focus on the local realities and arrangements of power within the respective geography and political configuration of each interviewee, which may be similar, but tend to represent very distinct sites of engagement and conditions. The movements the women interviewed here are involved with are not necessarily "transborder," in the sense described by Blackwell, although some act on the international stage. Yet the complexity of long-standing oppressive patriarchal arrangements, which Blackwell enumerates surrounding intersectional identities, seems to unite all.

This perfunctory literature review presents a useful background for engaging what follows.

Organization and *Reencuentro*

The previous sections of this introduction describe the themes that unite and bring solidarity to Indigenous feminine voices. While compiling this volume, the elephant in my mind would not be quieted: how to organize and honor each of these voices? How not to reproduce the colonial privileging of North over South? How to avoid selecting one tribal nation over the others? How to avoid pitting Latin American civil war abuses against the urgency of the disappearances and homicides of native women in and around North American oil drilling sites and elsewhere? How to determine whether the Amazonian jungle or DAPL be heard first, or is language revitalization and cultural patrimony of superior import? Where does involvement with the *Change the Mascot* movement rank in comparison to being a global Native singer/performer of resistance? Should the illustrious Olympic athlete be placed in the limelight, imitating the modus operandi of commercialization and commodification in global markets? Should greater space be allocated to the erudite anthropologists and sociologists who could explicate and make manifest these implicit structures of racism or are those teaching in the chalkboard classroom more vital in their contribution? How to map the appropriate flow chart for this erupting volcano of harmonizing voices of resistance? Is the alignment of these conversations to be by geodetic survey markers, thematics, chronology, profession, age, or generation? Where does media, radio broadcasters, or documentary filmmakers' rate on the hierarchies of categorization? What other vectors am I not considering?

Overwhelmed by the weight of these Occidental orderings forcing privilege of one direction over another in hierarchical fashion, I sought consultation with transcribers, a curator, and several participants. This allowed for the redistribution of the weight of this project from my shoulders onto the vibrant *huipil* tapestry of the written page. Eventually I ordered the interviews around my own literal and virtual journey through Guatemala to Maine to Arizona to Argentina to Zoom.

Ideally this volume would be multi-dimensional in shape and temporality. That is to say, modeled after *Reciprocidad en el mundo Andino* by interviewee Kichwa Luz Maria de la Torre Amaguaña and her coauthor Carlos Sandoval—it would open on the front page as either the Spanish or turned over right side up on the Kichwa version, neither privileged. It might resemble the mask worn in the Kichwa Inti Raymi Solstice festival that bears two faces that represent night and day, or past and present, and combines Christian and Kichwa traditions. How to navigate this spatial predicament so inherent to Western academic linear intellectual tradition and its respective dichotomies?

Grappling with this quandary, I turned to my long-time colleague Luz Maria de la Torre Amaguaña. That conversation marked a watershed moment. Firmly entrenched in the concept of reciprocity in the Andean world as a central axis, she outlined the ways in which this process of interviewing and compiling imbued both the women and myself with mutual respect and trust. She referred to it as a "*re-encuentro*," a personal re-encounter with oneself and reconnection with others. She underscored the importance of my role in the process of reaching out and then compiling, was integral. I, the Western-trained academic, coalesced with the assertion of "I am" in the scope of inclusion. This evolved into a device for organizing my walk along what I consider a sacred path with the voices in this book. In so doing, there is a reciprocal and complementary encounter between individual and self on various levels.

There is a plurality of voices, a collective consciousness that is being disseminated here. It reflects various processes or approaches which all lead to the same objective: to make visible Indigenous women's experience from the Northern and Southern hemispheres of the Americas. Stepping through this doorway, over this threshold into time and context on two continents, allows us to gain a view of the role of these voices and an understanding of who they are in relation to the cataclysmic changes occurring in society around them. Although the volume is collective in nature, there is a singular dynamic and dialectic between individual and collective identity. The voices apply Western logic and occidental tools of analysis in tandem with traditional knowledge and lifeways to counter dominant paradigms and stereotypes. Individual history, social engagement, life narratives, and identity branch out from what Luz Maria hails is the robust trunk of their culture. The Indigenous worldview, a solid trunk, is singular, holistic, and mutually nourishing and common to all of them. The point of departure is the self-identification of Native women, a *terra firme*, which brings strength and clarity, firm ground from that place of origin, to claim and assert "I am."[62]

The interviewees here trace how they consolidate that identity, to which they bring assurance, fortitude, and security and from which they explore their projections of individuality. They honor their ancestors while passing the baton to the next generation. Older generation women who have been involved in change movements for decades provide a perspective over that long timeframe indirectly through brief quotes. Younger generation women receive this legacy with the mission of transforming consciousness and rewriting the grand narrative of Indigenous peoples, and women in particular, using their own words and perspective. The new generation (many of the interviewees are in their 20s) who have treasured and safeguarded that message, even through the dark veil of racism and discrimination, are bold and courageous in their forthrightness.

Why weave this tapestry of voices? This volume is a form of vindication or realignment of Native values that ties to the imagery of walking on a sacred path. Indigenous and non-native readers might walk together just as a tapestry brings together threads creating a full, dense carpet, or path, intrinsic to the soul—a path which cannot be walked alone. The tapestry and the strands from which it is woven interlaces threads from academia, culture, language, traditional knowledge systems, and corresponding paradigms of reciprocity, complementarity, and balance. One strand, the academic compiler (me), serves as the figurative first hand in the weaving process, the first step in this particular walk. I, and the voices presented here, hope that this is one way to help build collective consciousness of social justice in humanity.

The title "Walking on our Sacred Path" was not taken lightly. I fully appreciate the sacrosanct in Indigenous cultures of the Sacred Path. *Recovering the Sacred—The Power of Naming and Claiming* begins with a chapter on what is sacred, the role of recovering the sacred in the process of healing a community, and its centrality to Indigenous vitality and sustainability. In defining the consecrated, Winona LaDuke says it is: "a complex and intergenerational process… of preservation or destruction of places…determination of the fate of skeletons and artifacts…held against the will of their rightful inheritors…on how the past is understood and what the future might bring." The stakes are high and the greatest irony for the Native populations is that the integrity of what they ascribe as sacred has been and will be determined, or undermined, by "the government that has been responsible for doing everything in its power to destroy Native American cultures."[63] This must change.

In *Sacred Instructions*, Sherri Mitchell describes the set of instructions we each carry from birth that help "align my spiritual truth with my human experience." The sacred instructions guide us through a process of healing the wounds of "our shared history" and forming "a more humane pathway forward" on a trail of "transcendence of differences and weaving of diverse expressions into a tapestry that is harmonized and aligned with common purpose…intent on preserving the integrity of all life in a harmonious balance."[64] Thus, notions of what is sacred and the relationship to our future sustainability are paramount for First Peoples around the world.

The sacred is tied to place, people, lifeways, beliefs, precepts, and spiritual culture. It is reflected in relics and material artifacts. It is a path into our hearts, minds, and souls, of the most intimate nature. For many, the sacred is something coveted in secret, yet at this time and place in history and of enunciation, it might breach the intimate plane to make profane a distinct worldview. Carrying these voices onto the written page as individual and collective expressions, I have entered into their trust and am privileged to walk along this path with them following their footsteps and guidance. The secular role of an editor is based on these women having entrusted me to bring their voices to the printed page. I honor and respect these voices, their intellectual musings, and knowledge production about what has been unwritten and, in some cases, unspoken. We, I humbly insert myself as the editor—everyone who has collaborated in this project as transcribers, translators, and readers—walk with these agents of change, hoping to open windows and doors, to intertwine unknown patterns at this propitious time in history.

Our objective is, as Luz Maria says, to "*compaginar*"—make compatible and harmonious—literally get on the same page with one another. In the book's production and organic evolution, we nurture one another. We are educating, informing our intellectual and compassionate sides, nourishing, and growing mutually. For native cultures, mutuality and respect are held high on the moral coda underpinning their sacred practices. The binding that occurs is to one another as much as to the Earth. Dr. Henrietta Mann encourages this kind of action in a Sierra Club article "Sacred Landscapes:" "we have a spiritual responsibility to renew the Earth, and we do this through our ceremonies so that our Mother, the Earth, can continue to support us. Mutuality and respect are part of our tradition—give and take."[65] When we get on the same page with a view of sustainability and living the Good Life, a process surfaces which eclipses solely profit-driven material exploitation, accumulation, and, eventually, destruction. The sacred path on which we, as voices and readers, embark is one cleared in affirmation and mutual respect for humanity and the natural world. Although I am, by profession, an academic, this is not an endeavor of research so much as it is a collection of hymns, voices of people in a chorus to reach Good.

Interviewees

I encountered many women on this path. Some participated directly and are quoted by name. Others were part of the background research and information gathering process. In 2004, in Ecuador, I met Luz Maria de la Torre Amaguaña at the Fulbright Commission. Her lecture inspired my previous book on the representation of Indigenous women in Latin American letters, *Indigenous Feminist Narratives: I/We: Wo(man) of an(Other) Way*. My first interview with Luz Maria appeared in *Cultural Survival Quarterly* and later I included a translation of her journal article, "What It Means to Be an Indigenous Woman in Contemporary Times," in the aforementioned book.

This particular project jumpstarted in 2013 in Oaxaca, Mexico at an ERIP-LASA panel on Indigenous feminism, when I dined with several scholars, native and non-native, involved with, and interpreting Indigenous writing from Guatemala.

In 2016, Velásquez Nimatuj and De la Torre Amaguaña came to the University of Utah on a Dee grant to present a talk in the class series, "Indigenous Feminist Activism and Social Change." A few other Guatemalan Maya activists who are well-known for their protests were suggested to me as possible contacts.[66] In September 2017, after my lecture for a Women's Enrollment Initiative, Crystal Lynn Tulley-Cordova, then a geology doctoral student, approached me. As I described this book project, she not only agreed to participate, but also recommended a Maya United Nations colleague, who kindly accepted an invitation. We conducted that interview at a radio station in Guatemala, where she explained its mission and her role as Indigenous radio broadcaster. While there, I also met with Lucía Inés Xiloj Cuin, Maya K'iche' lawyer from Chichicastenango. Her professional profile focuses on restitution for victims of the genocide during the Guatemalan Civil War. Aura Estela Cumes Simon, a Ph.D. social anthropologist, met me for a second time in her home in Chimaltenango. Previously, I had interviewed her for *Indigenous Feminist Narratives I/We: Wo(man) of (an)Other Way*. Next, Liliana Hernandez, a Maya lawyer who defends victims of the civil war abuse, broached difficult topics related to her legal field. Maya Kaqchikel Juan Batzibal human rights defender requested the interview take place in Coban during a conference on Indigenous women's rights. We recorded between conference sessions.

From the north, I travelled back to Guatemala City, where Victoria Tubin, journalist and academic, met me at her classroom on the campus of USAC (Universidad de San Carlos de Guatemala). I then spoke with performer Sara

Curruchich. The trajectory of her coming into consciousness about that identity is relayed in her interview.

Home in Utah, I attended a lecture by Jacqueline Keeler, editor of *Edge of Morning Native Voices Speak for the Bears Ears*, and co-founder of *Eradicating Offensive Native Mascotry.*[67] Keeler traced the sovereign claims and rights of the First Nations on tribal lands which have been settled and stolen. Later that day, while having dinner with James Singer, a Navajo sociologist and 2018 Utah Congressional candidate, my thoughts veered toward contacting Native American change makers in the United States and Canada. Singer steered me to activists involved in DAPL and Bears Ears, some of whom are quoted in this book. Franci Taylor, recent director of the American Indian Resource Center (AIRC), talked with me about the overall project and, although she declined participation[68], she guided me to Davina Dah Yi'itihi Smith. She also suggested looking at the trailblazing litigation against mascots and appropriation in sports and commercial enterprise. A conversation with one person led to a proverbial village of activist Indigenous women.

Soon thereafter, a plaintiff involved in an anti-mascot lawsuit convened our meeting at a café in Arizona and described activism in the anti-mascot movement. At that time, I was introduced to Callan Chythlook-Sifsof, a United States Olympic Snowboard team member.

In fall 2017, President Trump decided to reduce the size of the Bears Ears National Monument. There were peaceful protests at the Utah State Capitol. In an unprecedented manner, several Native tribes combined forces to protest this action in public and legal law suits. Cassandra Begay, a board member of Pandos, an environmental and Native rights group, was among the activists. She declined to participate in these conversations because of personal trauma and her transition out of front-line activism. However, her important voice has been featured in conversation with President Obama in *Live Desk with President Barack Obama at Obama Foundation Summit in Chicago*. Samantha Eldridge, currently on the Executive Staff for the Navajo Nation Office of the President and Vice President for liaison to Utah, briefly touched base with me around that time as well.

Beyond the local area, I was referred to a member of Honor the Earth by correspondence with Winona LaDuke, who declined participation. That interview was conducted by phone from a car as this individual travelled to DAPL.

A more detailed biography for each of the women who have given permission to appear by name or anonymously appears before the extracts from their interviews in the following chapter.

Finally, two activist women, both quite well-known, spent hours conversing with me: Rebecca Adamson and Honorable Donna M. Loring. Here, they both play a distinct role—their voices are interspersed throughout and provide a seasoned perspective on Native People's rationale and approach to transformation.

I visited libraries holding their archives. Through examination of the personal papers, written speeches, correspondence, and other items housed in special collections, I hoped to garner a sense of Adamson's, Loring's, and also LaDuke's, individual and collective definitions of resistance during the 1970s and 1980s. The objective was to hone a comparative study of Native North American female public intellectuals from their personal writings about resistance work in relation to their identity as Indigenous women. Specifically, I wanted to consider how their attitudes and actions contrast and harmonize regarding activism today from their initial interventions during 1970–2000.

Representative Loring, who is retired, was a First Nations Band representative to the Maine Legislature for tribal Penobscot members. She was appointed in 2019 as Senior Advisor on Tribal Affairs to Governor Janet Mills of Maine. The Maine Women Writers Collection, University of New England, holds her papers. Her contributions in the political domain bring an important mainstream branch of resistance work and offer a distinct perspective. Meeting at her home in Maine, reading her books and poring through her papers raised questions: How did she advocate for her community in her legislative role? How does she embrace resistance, frame this daunting task, and negotiate, even advocate, as a representative, within the hegemonic seats of power in the US? What personal and professional struggles were endured in Vietnam and as legislator as Native American woman? Loring's experience sheds crucial light on the efficacy and challenge of functioning as collaborator and resistance agent within bureaucratic governing institutions of power.

Rebecca Adamson is currently retired from the national organizations she founded for Indian education and economic development opportunities. Her impressive credentials and significant interventions with the Native American communities are documented online, in video recordings,[69] and in hard copy. The Smith College-Sofia Smith Special Collection holds extensive and comprehensive Adamson papers. The majority of her work was in real-time activism—founding institutes and promulgating training for self-sufficient development proposals in Native communities. Her philosophy rethinks and establishes educational opportunities and schools outside of the violently abusive Indian boarding school system that traumatized Native children. Other projects draw from her business background to provide microloan investments and open monetary channels for the comprehensive social and economic impact on the reservations, based on native designs. She has conducted scholarly research analyzing the economics of Native self-sufficiency and subsistence economies, rethinking Occidental investment/divestment strategies and development models in diverse contested areas like the Amazonian jungle, DAPL, and other environmentally-sensitive yet lucrative natural resource extraction enterprises.[70]

As an Indigenous economist, Adamson is a singular role model for Native women. Yet, when one refers to this iconic status in her capacity as a Native female economist, she replies, "I am like a sole pea under a mattress."[71] She is not alone in her struggles to bring social justice and equality of resources and opportunities—transforming consciousness about what Indigenous development could look like. Few women with Native ties have had or have her educational background in the field of finance and economics. Her track record of accomplishments and accolades thus merit our attention. Adamson brings an activist Indigenous economics to bear on self-determination. Hers is a vital voice, because of her professional training, experience, and ability to articulate so clearly what can be done in economic terms—and how this system has failed or seen success. She and Loring complement the younger women interviewed here, who work within and outside of establishment in significant ways as adept sophisticated envoys of struggle and solidarity.

There are other women I spoke with in conversations around their shifting roles from front-line activism and professional engagement in other realms. Among these is Larissa Fast Horse, playwright and founder of *Indigenous Direction*—a consulting firm for companies and artists who want to create accurate work about, for, and with Indigenous Peoples. Another, Charlotte "Carol" Surveyor, a 2018 Democratic candidate to the U.S. House, 2nd Congressional District of Utah. She co-founded the Utah League of Native American Voters. Her experience and insight infuse this project indirectly.

Within the academy there are two profound examples I witnessed of Indigenous women's empowerment and rhetorical activist intervention. The first occurred at CLACSO (Latin American Social Science Thinktank) 2018 Buenos Aires, in the panel "Plurinational States and *Buen Vivir* as a Right: A Critical Take from Women Who Struggle." Speakers Moira Millan (Mapuche social activist), Irma Caupan (Mujeres Originarias por el Buen Vivir, Argentina), Juana Kuante (Lonko Mapuche-Williche and Spokes person for Alianza Territorial), Xochitl Leyva Solano (Centro de Investigación y Estudios Superiores en Antropología Social, México) addressed the audience. Relegated to a small classroom only large enough to hold fifteen people, the panel refused to continue in that limited space where people were sardined in to the point that wheel-chair-bound panelist Mercedes Oliveira was unable to access the room to participate. Halting the proceedings, Millan and the panel took over the basement floor of the Cultural Center, standing on the stairs without a microphone as they continued to present their session. With more than 100 people in attendance, Millan explained the need not to normalize the marginalization, invisibilization, or silencing of Indigenous women, who necessarily needed to be afforded their place at this 7,000-person academic conference organized by the quintessential think-tank of Latin American Social Sciences. Banners around the city, with the logo "More rights, less privilege," decried the CLACSO gathering as a counter-response to the G20 meeting, which would take place the following week. The panelists enunciated a forceful denunciation of the brutal violent measures occurring against the Mapuche on their lands in Argentina and Chile, decrying multinational corporations' exploitation of the Indigenous People and their resources.

Secondly, a keynote speech by Dr. Pam Palmater at LASA-ERIP 2019 (Latin American Studies-Ethnicity, Race and Indigenous Peoples) reveals the ongoing commitment and logic of resistance by Indigenous People. Palmater's books, *Warrior Life* and *Beyond Blood*, promote activism and consultation, seek legal status and recourse, and redefine identity beyond the gender discrimination of descent-based rules for legal and constitutional enfranchisement. She speaks directly on the dire situation of missing Native women in Western Canada and the United States, as well as the illegal arrests of land defenders against pipeline construction.

I am grateful to every one of these individuals for our conversations. I respect the transparency of these women about their past activism and present needs to revitalize and rekindle their energy, whether interviewed to be included here or not—many cited personal challenges, especially around the continuing disappearance of and violence endured by Native women everywhere. For some, the book has provided an outlet to voice this pain and sadness. Together we are bushwhacking a path towards freedom and respect.

Structure of Book and Chapters

These interviews, which took place from November 2016 through Fall 2018, are transcribed in excerpts (and translations from Spanish where necessary). Following the introduction, Chapter 2 includes the responses to the initial questions on identity and activism. These delve into the definitions and characterization of

Indigenous and Native American activism as informed by identity. Chapter 3 provides a historical context of the so-called "Indian Problem," and an overview of State policies instituted in North and South America regarding Native People's rights. Although the term "problem" is in disuse generally in the twenty-first century, there is a charged legacy of presuming the Indigenous Peoples are "the" problem to national development with which theorists, policy makers, and practitioners must contend. The consensus of the women interviewed here is that the colonizer's trope be laid to rest and a paradigm shift occur in order for there to be an equitable and sustainable future on Earth for all people. Chapter 4 transcribes the most poignant responses from interviewees on the topic of Native People as "problem." Chapter 5 highlights the responses to the question of the role of social sciences in a time when the methodology of the study of human and social interaction has been biased and compromised. Chapter 6 transcribes the self-representation of "what it means to be an Indigenous woman today" from the perspective of these women actively seeking change.

Notes

1 Epigraph sources, in sequence: Chúngara de Barrios (1977), Thompson (1991), and Zitkala Sa; Menchú (1983).
2 Thompson, *To the American Indian*, xxx.
3 Thompson, *To the American Indian*, 1.
4 *New York Times*, "Obituary."
5 Zitkala Sa, MS1704.
6 Beverley, John, "Testimonio, Subalternity, and Narrative Authority," 555–565.
7 Gugelberger, *The Real Thing*, 1–19.
8 Döring, *Postcolonial Literatures in English*, 69.
9 Menchú, *I, Rigoberta Menchú*, 1.
10 Spivak, *Can the Subaltern Speak*.
11 Chúngara de Barrios, *Let Me Speak!*, 19.
12 Living Justice Press, "Elizabeth Cook-Lynn."
13 Davina Dah Yi'itihi Smith, in discussion with the author, November 9, 2017.
14 Florio, *Broken Rainbow*.
15 Smith, discussion.
16 Liliana Hernandez, in discussion with the author, September 28, 2017.
17 Finley, "Viola Davis' Powerful Speech for Women of Color at the Women's March."
18 Aura Cumes, in discussion with the author, September 23, 2017.
19 Lucia Xiloj, in discussion with the author, September 24, 2017.
20 Callan Chythlook-Sifsof, in discussion with the author, October 10, 2017.

21 Hernandez, discussion.
22 Interview with Liga Maya staff member, discussion with author in confidentiality, name withheld by mutual agreement, September 25, 2017.
23 Houska, "The Standing Rock Resistance and Our Fight for Indigenous Rights."
24 Public denunciation of the death threats against Indigenous listed herein: "Consejería de Derechos de los Pueblos, DDHH Y PAZ Organización Nacional Indígena de Colombia ONIC 27 de octubre de 2017 NIT. 860.521.808-1 Denuncia pública amenaza de muerte contra dirigentes indígenas Aida Quilcué Vivas, Feliciano Valencia, Hermes Pete, Fabián Molcué y Alveiro Mamaño. La Consejería de Derechos de los Pueblos Indígenas, DDHH y Paz de la ONIC denuncia a la opinión pública nacional e internacional, la amenaza de muerte emitida en las últimas horas contra los compañeros y compañeras Feliciano Valencia, Aida Qulque Vivas, Alveiro Mamaño y Hermes Pete, dirigentes indígenas procedentes del Cauca y quienes adelantan acciones por la defensa de los derechos de los pueblos indígenas y la defensa del territorio a nivel departamental y nacional," posted by Dr. Joanne Rappaport, Professor Georgetown University on ERIP-listserv.
25 *Cultural Survival Quarterly*, "Indigenous Women Rising."
26 *Global Witness*, 2021.
27 Transparency International, "Corruptions, Perceptions."
28 Reporters Without Borders, *World Press Freedom Index*; Freedom House, *Freedom on the World.*
29 Simpson, 2016.
30 Simpson, 2016.
31 Interview with Indigenous environmental organization staff member, discussion with author in confidentiality, name withheld by mutual agreement, November 15, 2016.
32 Simpson, interview by Naomi Klein, 2013.
33 Marin in discussion with the author, November 21, 2017.
34 LaDuke, interview by Jennifer Arlen, 1980.
35 Curruchich, in discussion with the author, September 26, 2017.
36 Interview with DAPL protest organizer, discussion with author in confidentiality, name withheld by mutual agreement, November 15, 2016.
37 Fernández Benítez, *Íkala*, 2010, 47–71.
38 LaDuke, "Minobimaatisiiwin—the good life."
39 Taylor, in discussion with the author, 2016.
40 Rechtshaffen, "Powerful 500 years."
41 Colectiva#SOS, "Irma Velasquez Nimatuj."
42 IMDb, https://www.imdb.com/title/tt6098512.
43 Ensler, *Vagina Monologues.*
44 LaDuke, "Minobimaatisiiwin—the good life."
45 Adamson, "Global Activism for Indigenous People".

46 Loring, *In the Shadow of the Eagle*, 140.
47 Pacari, interview by Iñaki Makazaga, 2017.
48 *Cultural Survival*, 1992.
49 Wauneka, *I'll Go and Do More*, 208.
50 Microaggressions: "quotidian verbal, nonverbal, and environmental slights, snubs, or insults, whether intentional or unintentional, which communicate hostile, derogatory, or negative messages to target persons based solely upon their marginalized group membership" *Psychology Today*, 2010.
51 Steiner, *New Indians*, 225.
52 Wauneka, *I'll Go and Do More*, 245.
53 LaDuke, "Seeds of Our Ancestors."
54 Ouellette, *The Fourth World*, 11–12.
55 Hawkesworth, *Globalization and Feminist Activism*, 25, 37.
56 Feree, *Global Feminism*, vii, xxi.
57 Naples, *Women's activism and globalization*.
58 Juris, *Insurgent Encounters*; Lagalisse, "Marginalizing Magdalena;" Maier, *Women's Activism in Latin America and the Caribbean*; Krouse, *Keep the Campfires Going*; Hallum-Montes, "A Shared Responsibility."
59 Hargreaves, *Violence Against Indigenous Women*, 65.
60 Stephen, "Indigenous Women and Violence."
61 Cultural Survival Quarterly, "A Decade of Cultural Survival Quarterly."
62 The metaphor of the tree and trunk were elaborated by De la Torre Amaguaña in the cited interview. She also referred to the concept of *terra firme*.
63 LaDuke, *Recovering the Sacred—The Power of Naming and Claiming*, ii, 24.
64 Mitchell, *Sacred Instructions*, ix, xx.
65 Taliman, *Sacred Landscapes*.
66 I reached out to various women suggested during an exchange with a colleague: Miriam Pixtun (La Puya anti-gold mining movement); Juana Sales (Tz'ununija Indigenous Women's Movement-"branded enemy of the State"); Crisanta Perez Bimaca (Maya Mam anti-Canada's Goldcorp Inc); and Gladys Tzul Tzul (Maya K'iche' sociologist).
67 Keeler, of Diné and Yankton Dakota heritage, is a prolific writer for the Nation. Her lecture was part of the Westminster Heritage Speakers series, given on Indigenous People's day, October 13, 2017. She traced the sovereignty claims and rights of the Nations on tribal lands which have been settled and stolen.
68 Taylor offered the following suggestions amongst others: Cinnamon (Spears) Kills First (Northern Cheyenne, word warrior); Dr. Henriettta Mann (Cheyenne, academic), FNX (First Nations Experience- national broadcast television network); Marie Batiste (Potlotek First Nation and Micmac, Canada, academic); Jo-Ann Archibald – Q'um Q'um Xiiem (Sto:lo First Nation, scholar and educator); Kim Anderson (Cree/Métis, writer and educator, Canada, Life Stages and Native Women

Memory, Teachings, and Story Medicine, 2011); Holly Young (Dakota, artist and beadwork); Madonna Thunder Hawk (Oohenumpa band of the Cheyenne River Sioux, founder AIM American Indian Movement); Yvonne Swan Wanrow (Sinixt/Colville Native American, activist); Tipiziwin Tolman (Lakhota, educator and-artist); Lori Arviso Alvord (Dine', surgeon); Felicia Bartley (Pueblo of Isleta, fashion designer), Radmilla Cody (Navajo, recording artist), Meghann O'Brien, (Haida/Kwakwaka'wakw weaver), and Yolanda Francisco-Nez (Navajo/Dine', Executive Director Ancestral Winds).

69 See, for instance, Makers 2017; TED MED 2018; "Enoughness: Indigenous Economics 101" 2016.

70 Women's Media Center, Rebecca Adamson profile; also, Moyers, "Making Change".

71 Adamson, in discussion with the author, 2018.

2 Identity and Activism

This chapter renders excerpts from the interviews regarding questions posed on self-identification and activism. The point of departure in our discussions was the enunciation of one's identity. Indigenous women have been represented, spoken for, demeaned, and their bodies appropriated throughout Western history and letters, even as they play a central role in their tribal community, home, and on the protest front. Therefore, it was important to start our conversations with their self-representation. The topic generated unique, yet nearly parallel, patterns of response, which effectively demonstrates the tight relationship that exists between Indigenous identity and activism. In particular, the nature of Indigenous roots and cultural claims to identity informs these women's lives, choices, and personal resistance work. Although the women come from disparate geographical and figurative sites, and have varied professional profiles, their self-portraits reflect local nuances and commonalities. Several common threads emerge to unite their self-portraits.

Identity

I introduce the interviewees in the order in which I encountered them, as that path materialized through interconnections and as one encounter led to another. The brief biography situates them on a European timeline with a professional curriculum vitae, which contrasts with their own articulations of who they are.

Although there are individual portraits here, Indigenous women's identity is not monolithic nor homogenous. The assertions here will show distinctions and, certainly, some come from more privilege.

> I identify myself as a Maya Quiché woman, originating from the urban center, a family of merchants, and coming from a sector that has had access to educational opportunities, financed by my parents. I have had access to healthcare, and good nutrition, extraordinary privilege, to which most Indigenous peoples are not privy. In addition, my training has taken place among Indigenous leaders, as well as non-natives, foreigners, ladinos, mestizos, and many others. Because of all this privilege and access, I developed the critical awareness that I have today.[1]

Luz Maria de la Torre came to Utah in 2005 on a Dee Teaching Grant for my class on *Indigeneity in Latin American letters*. At that time, she was the Quechua instructor at Arizona State University. In 2016, she returned to Utah for a public lecture and classroom intervention as part of Indigenous women's activism grant. Since 2009, she has been a Continuing Lecturer at UCLA. Her BA in Languages and Applied Linguistics from Catholic University of Ecuador produced ground-breaking research on Indigenous Bilingual Education. She completed a Master's degree in Political Sciences at *Facultad Latinoamericana de Ciencias Sociales* (FLACSO) in 2006. Her publications focus on bilingual education, the history of Indigenous women from Otavalo, the Ecuadorian Indigenous Movement during the 1990s, Indigenous concepts of reciprocity and knowledge production, as well as gender informed by an Andean perspective.

> I am Luz María de la Torre Amaguaña. My nationality is Kichwa, from the Otavalo Pueblo in Ecuador. In terms of gender, society and the practices of quotidian colonialism, [these forces] have inscribed notions of gender and corresponding behaviors associated with being a woman upon me, and so I consider myself a woman. I am female.[2]

As an educator, she understands the role of Indigenous scholars within the system as representatives of a marginalized ethnic group. She reflects on the impact of her identity in allowing students to grapple directly with concepts often only treated in theory.

> It is crucial within academic circles that we, Indigenous women, express ourselves with our own voices. Indeed, imagine the difference it makes on a student to hear about these topics from a non-native, albeit with passion, enthusiasm and confidence. Whereas, when we stand up in front of them, in a space to which we have not been privy, the grave responsibility to express our lives within the academic realm becomes unique and formidable. To a certain degree this would be a change in the known paradigm; a great achievement that could mutually nourish us. The ultimate challenge is to find strategies to communicate this concept to a non-native audience. I have spent my professional life interacting with leaders and trainers, and likewise training them. We, as Indigenous, all experienced the same process.
>
> It is wholly another thing to be here in the States, educating those unfamiliar with my culture and our circumstances. We offer them tools, strategies, and education about something truly unknown. However, one of the most empowering acts of our endeavors is testimonial, because there is no mediation, purely our words. Simply put, this is what we have lived. It is characteristic of the way to open new spaces: as Indigenous, professionals, where our words are listened to, respected, and most importantly replicated in each of our experiences.
>
> Furthermore, we would never approach someone else and tell them: "we have your answer. Do this!" The answer will have to come from within. It is similar to our typical dances—we dance next to each other, opposite and all around. Slowly we come together and then recede, getting closer and then moving apart. It is a way to fall in love, to find things in common, and to abandon differences. Finding common ground has high costs—you have to give up some things also. We don't have a recipe that says "Step one, you have to start this way." No, what must prevail is primarily sincerity, that spirit, that reality of participating in events that must be changed. Because we cannot live with hypocrises, which is what's hurting us now.[3]

Crystal Tulley-Cordova was a doctoral candidate at the University of Utah in the Department of Geology and Geophysics, completing a dissertation on water resources in the Navajo Nation.[4] Today she is Principal Hydrologist for the Navajo Nation. In this capacity, she is involved with several groundbreaking projects with tribal, state, and federal partners. Her work involves actively participating in water rights settlement on behalf of her tribe. She is a proud mother of two, including her daughter Baahozhoni, translated as *Happy One/Warrior Woman who treads with balance in all things.*

> My Name is Crystal Tulley-Cordova. I identify by saying Crystal Tulley-Cordova Tódích'íi'niinishłį́ Ta'neeszahnii bashishchiin Hashk'aa hadzohi eí dashicheii To'aheedliinii eí dashinalí. Those are my matrilineal clans; how I identify where I come from. I am of the Bitter Water Clan, born for the Tangle Clan. My maternal grandfather's clan is the Yucca Fruit-Strung-Out-in-a-Line. My paternal grandfather's clan is The Water Flows Together. The way I identify myself is not the norm. There's no bubble or slot that I'd be put in based on who I am and where I've come from.
>
> I grew up on the Navajo Nation, which is the largest land-based tribe in the United States. Growing up there, poverty is high, unemployment is high and, a lot of times, coming from those types of areas, you're not represented well outside the boundaries of the reservation because they identify you based on the statistics. Economically, you're put in this general pot of being less than, or less fortunate. However, my identity is very rich. Not in the sense of economic worth, having a lot of property, a lot of money, things that are important to a lot of people out there in the world. But I am rich in the sense that I know who I am and where I am from and where I am going.
>
> I have a large support system that helps me to get to where I am destined to go. That support system, well, I count my wealth like my grandpa used to count his wealth and that's by his family members and friends. So, I am a wealthy person.[5]

Crystal had collaborated with Maya contacts at the International Indigenous Women's Forum-Indigenous Women's Global Leadership School, and also participated in the United Nations Permanent Forum on Indigenous Issues 14th Session. This led me to one contact in Guatemala.

Poqomam media reporter Antonia Benito transmits in her native tongue at Radio Qawinaquel, an organization described as a "place of community" where she conducts interviews with locals in order to highlight environmental destruction, megaprojects, health and social challenges to the Indigenous, and disseminate information to empower Poqomam community members. Her discussion of "community" activism and identity binds the radio organization to the ethnic community as mutually supportive.

> In terms of economics, each of the communities manages from within its own space. We do this in the Qawinaqel organization as well, in a way that allows us to publicize the work that the people do. The women within communities [of ethnic affiliation] manage their own economy by making our traditional clothing, among other things, which is an important factor still managed from within our communities.

> We may not actually use the word "activist," but the people do, and the way the people perceive activism is determined by what we do. I cannot say that I am an activist if the people that surround me do not see it that way. If they do begin to see it that way, it's because the work we are developing in our communities is going well, and happening in such a way that they identify with what we do and the role that we are taking.
>
> Resistance is inherent to the work that we do both in terms of communication and organization. We try to maintain our own way of looking at life based on the Mayan cosmovision. It is a worldview of continuous resisting, of using our traditional clothing (which you can see as we walk freely along the streets), of using our native language wherever we are. Because if things were still like they were twenty years ago, our language, our own way of viewing life, the participation of Mayan women in different spaces might have already disappeared, but we are involved in the daily, quotidian vindication task of trying to keep this type of participation alive and to strengthen it.[6]

In 2017 Benito participated in Mexico on the forum "Empowerment of Indigenous Women for the eradication of hunger and malnutrition in Latin America and the Caribbean," which combined efforts by the Fund for the Development of Indigenous Peoples of Latin America and the Caribbean (FILAC, in Spanish) and the UN Food and Agriculture Organization (FAO). In 2022, she attended the XV World Forestry Conference. She is featured in "I'X Mujer Montaña" (2020) directed by Wanda López Trelles, a short film. In addition, her recent advocacy promotes protection of reporters, integration of women into the field of journalism, and opening media to non-Spanish speaking communities.

Lucía Xiloj has been committed to legal casework that challenges the criminalization of Indigenous men and women defenders of their territory. She is an advocate for victims of sexual assault during the war, and has appeared before the Guatemalan Supreme Court in litigious battles regarding the constitutionality of the right to prior consultation in matters pertaining to Indigenous territories. She has argued for the legal implementation of ILO 169, the 1989 Indigenous and Tribal Peoples Convention, precursor to the Declaration of Indigenous Peoples Rights. Her professional profile includes work as a consultant with Oxfam, Waqib' Kej and the judicial court system.

> My name is Lucía Xiloj. I am a Maya Quiché woman. My whole family is of Quiché descent. I am from Chichicastenango. I am also a lawyer. In this field, I am currently helping several women, especially in gaining access to justice for severe sexual abuse that they suffered during the Guatemalan Civil War. Many

women were objects of sexual violence and, unfortunately, throughout the peace process, the topic of women and the violence they suffered has been left invisibilized and erased.

Approximately ten years ago it began to come to light that women were in fact victims of severe sexual violence, and important steps have been taken in the justice system in that regard. But it is still necessary to continue with this work, because in our racist and misogynist society, these women are often not believed.

It is important to continue with these processes to show that these were not isolated incidents, but rather part of what was practically a national policy which was seen almost everywhere in the country—where there were massacres, women were also raped. We want women to be able to continue becoming stronger, and to be considered subjects of law, because in our societies, oftentimes even in the Indigenous communities, women are only considered objects, even though there is a romantic perception that everything is going well.

I came to study here in the capital city when I was fourteen years old, because my father was one of the few people who believed that women also had the right to receive an education. He wanted me to receive a quality education, which is why he sent me to study in Guatemala City when I was young.

I started becoming involved in the educational world, and prior to that time, I had never realized how racist Guatemala was (and is), because I grew up in Chichicastenango, whose population is primarily Quiché, and was never aware of the racist relations that existed in the rest of the country.

I became aware of this complicated situation when I arrived here in the capital, and what gave me the strength to continue studying, and even to vindicate myself as a woman (though I did not have the political consciousness to know what that meant) was my mother's support.

When I was in school, they wanted me to wear the school uniform, the justification being that I would feel bad or uncomfortable in my traditional clothing. I was debating with myself, "is it better if I put it on or not…" but then my mother told me, "don't feel ashamed of your clothing." It was a kind of shock when she told me that, because at that moment I was under that impression that I *would* feel ashamed, but as soon as she said that everything changed. I felt more empowered to say no. I would not wear the uniform.

I continued wearing my traditional clothing, and when I was able to study at the university, the burden of racism continued. Now that I am a professional, it is even more present, because on the street and in other places nobody can imagine that I might have a profession in the university.

I helped with a case of discrimination against a woman who worked in the courts. The representative of the Public Ministry looked at *her* instead of me, and said, "oh, you're a lawyer?" when in fact, *I* was the lawyer. This always happens when we don our traditional clothing. It is a form of stereotyping, and that is why it is important to me to have a symbol for this political recognition that I am an Indigenous woman, but that I can also have other options in life.[7]

Aura Estela Cumes Simon completed her doctoral thesis under the direction of Dr. Rosalba Aida Hernandez at Centro de Investigaciones y Estudios Superiores en Antropología Social (CIESAS). Her 2014 study is *The "Indian" Woman as "Servant." Domestic Service, Colonialism and Patriarchy in Guatemala.* She has published extensively and is a consultant for organizations that empower Indigenous women. She describes her coming into consciousness about her identity, discrimination, and activism through everyday experience and Bible study.

I was interviewed by an online journal called *Plaza Pública*. I thought about my activism, which is not an organized activism, but one which begins with the mechanism of being able to rebel against various forms of racism. As a child I did not call it "racism," because this term has only been used recently within Maya political action. We used terms such as disdain, humiliation, and mistreatment, which we received on a daily basis.

My activism begins when I go to the market and someone calls me a "piece of shit Indian." I do not accept that. From there I rebel, even though rebelling in situations where you have no power is complicated. When I used to rebel against the *ladina* woman who ran a store, I had little chance of winning, because the *ladinos* hold the power that is reserved exclusively for non-Indigenous in this country.

For that reason, rebelling when I was a child also led to the consequence of stronger aggression against me. I remember my sister in those moments. She would tell me, "you shouldn't react, because it will be worse for you." Yet I recall my activism was ignited there. My activism did not begin with the consciousness building that took place later, just in that moment.

My activism as a woman initiated when I was allowed to play an important role in the Bible School. I knew that I could do what they asked of us, which was to learn alongside males. I was also aware that when one is an adolescent, there is a separation in which it is the men who speak for the women, based on the biblical passage that states that women are to be quiet in the congregation because they are not allowed to speak. At that point, I began to wonder (as any human being would do under those conditions) how it was possible that those boys (who moreover were slower when it came to learning) would come to speak for us, simply because they were males. These are the things that cause me not to accept the conditions in which I exist. My activism is structured there.[8]

Cumes stresses the individuality of choices and heterogeneity of Indigenous women's identity and activism. She reiterates the notion that activism can take many forms, including indirect questioning of the system, open protest, and supporting the intercultural premise of modernity.

> After we signed the peace agreement [1996] I found myself in organizations that are designed as Maya, and with women's organizations as well. When I hear the purpose of their struggle articulated, I realize that to a large extent they involve something that I have been doing by myself. I rarely work for Indigenous organizations. If anything, I am closer to women's organizations, but my activism continues to be largely individual.[9]

Juana Batzibal, an anthropologist with the Center for Legal Action on Human Rights (CALDH) in Guatemala City, publishes articles on racism against Indigenous peoples in Guatemala and cross-sectionality of Indigenous identity, gender, and ethnicity.[10] She reflects in those writings on how identity and activism are grounded in the tenets of ancestral justice and indigenous values, though specific to the individual.

Indigenous resurgence for some will involve connecting with their own cultural traditions and simultaneously with the contemporary struggles of other groups. Leanne Simpson sees the alliances that can be forged:

> In terms of solidarity, I'm interested in nurturing a closer and more generative relationship with people in my territory. So I'm asking myself questions like how do I live in solidarity with Black Lives Matter? What does Nishnaabewin say my responsibilities are in terms of sharing land and space with Black communities imaging other worlds? How can I understand colonialism if I do not understand the Black scholars' theoretical brilliance in understanding slavery? How am I listening to and supporting Indigenous trans people? How am I connecting my own struggle with colonialism to the rest of the world, [including] the plant and animal nations? How am I acting in solidarity with Lake Ontario? Those questions are much more important to me, and I think when we center that, authentic and ethical allies come onboard anyway.[11]

A Maya researcher voices certain ambivalence about assuming the term activist, since the definitions are personal for each woman.

> I do identify myself as an activist, yes and no. We assume two and three roles at once. In my condition of being a woman, one contributes by way of research and training. In the case of Guatemala in particular (due to the dynamic that is born from the defense of territory and Mother Earth), naturally we are engaged

in activism. Also, we need to manifest political proposals for structural changes in this State in which we are living.

As you may realize, today increasingly there is much turmoil confronting our governing bodies and individual citizens, equally so in the legislative bodies as well as in the executive. There is a fissure that begins with the State structure and the Nation.

In Guatemala, there is a state without a nation, whereas there has been a nation without a state for a while. That state, which is constituted from the Greco-Roman model, does not correspond (nor respond) to a nation that is based on a holistic and cosmogonic way of thinking. There has been a fundamental clash, from the moment of political and legal development, during the period of creating laws and codes, wherein the entire population of the Indigenous People, were excluded permanently from the process.

Regardless whether one is Maya, Garífuna o Xinka, or one of our *mestizo* brothers who live in poverty or in rural areas, no one was included. That marginalization obliges us in many circumstances to have to engage in activism, but we cannot separate or isolate activism exclusively within the political realm, or within research or training. We must imagine our contributions in this permanent battle in a more integrated way. For this reason, I see myself as an activist 100%, yet I also detach from the term activism. I am a social anthropologist.[12]

Victoria Tubin, journalist and academic, has published several important pieces in *Plaza Pública* in Guatemala. Her articles explore the central issues of "What it means to be a woman and Maya."[13] She was an adjunct professor at Universidad de San Carlos de Guatemala (USAC)—one of only three Indigenous scholars on the faculty.

I am Victoria Aurora Tubin, Maya Kaqchikel. I am a professional woman, graduate in sociology, as well as having obtained a Masters in communications and development studies. I am completing a doctorate in social sciences.

With respect to gender, I consider myself a Maya woman. I oppose patriarchal paradigms because they oppress Maya women, generating a series of injustices against women. I do not consider myself feminist, rather as a woman who fights to make visible the injustices that Indigenous women face.

As an example, our quest for the vindication of the struggle that recognizes First Peoples is foremost and this mainly because our history has been distorted and misrepresented. We have, and are told a history which is not ours.

For that reason, I discuss concepts, among which is ethnicity, an abstract word that does not embody or reflect one of the key problems which we, First Peoples (particularly women), face of racism.

Racism is a problem that encompasses much more than just ethnicity, since it stems from concepts of race, inferiority, and subordination of some people or one group, while others are elevated and considered superior to them. This has to do with power relations.

The discussion revolves around our positioning ourselves in a global era and context, a phenomenon impacting Indigenous Peoples more than others, because there is an overriding push to globalize everything without taking into account the particular conduct, lifeways, and ways of interacting with nature. In this manner, those involved in resistance work have been able to enter the conversation.

A sense of defiance has been passed down through generations, beginning with the resistance to the invasion of the Spaniards. Undoubtedly, we have experienced tremendous moments of violence, most notably the last one during the internal armed conflict of our civil war. Now we are in another phase of the global era, with the continuation of development models imposed from afar, yet what we strive for is the insertion of new development projects, that are geared to the pueblo and the people, instead of for the benefit of a few.

The prevailing model of development has brought with it a series of destructions, especially of our identity, our livelihood, our existence as First People, our relationship with the land and earth, and the universe. Most importantly, it has caused a loss of our identity as First Peoples.[14]

Sara Curruchich is a guitarist and singer who performs in her native tongue, appearing around the globe and online in various social media platforms. She defends the rights of women and Indigenous People. Her performances are featured in films, online platforms, and podcasts[15]. She is in her twenties and has reclaimed her identity as an Indigenous woman with pride and protest. Many of her songs, sung in Spanish and Kakchiquel, such as *Resistir* and *Ralk'walUlew, Hijas e Hijos de la Tierra* [Sons and Daughters of the Earth],[16] have been distributed globally and may be found on YouTube and other social media platforms. *Ralk'walUlew* is performed in Pamela Yates' documentary, *500 Years*. Her comments depict the contradictions felt by individuals who have grown up in a racist society under a colonial mindset that disparages and instills shame for the oppressed culture. With consciousness of the perverse consequences of colonization, she embraces her identity and its cultural trappings.

I am an Indigenous Maya woman from San Juan Comalapa, Chimaltenango, one of the many First Peoples affected during the internal conflict in Guatemala. I am 24 years old, though in a way my personal development and identity formation have required deliberate thought. To some extent, my development has even been truncated, given my background growing up here in Guatemala as an Indigenous person.

To speak about my identity, as well as about being part of an ethnic group, of an Indigenous People, bears great weight and complexity. This identity carries with it formidable challenges, such as racism and discrimination, which are prevalent in our country and around the world.

In Guatemala, even though the majority of the population is Indigenous, racism and discrimination toward the Indigenous people is ubiquitous as expressed by many non-Native individuals in our nation-state. That discrimination and racism sets us apart into disparate, inequitable stations of life. Most Indigenous populations do not have schools or health centers; and do not have, in many places, something as basic as the three distinct food groups, for example. That discrimination leads to Indigenous people unwillingly having to assume a lower socio-economic rank, not because we want to be or should be, but because we are denied participation in terms of work, opportunities, and access to resources.

I have undergone a process of strengthening my identity as an Indigenous person, and in particular, of being a Maya woman, descendant of grandmothers and grandparents. My process of reinvigorating my identity has been similar to that of many other women who have encountered these obstacles.

Personally, I spent a year in which I felt ashamed to identify myself as an Indigenous woman. This was not intentional self-rejection, rather because I was forced to come to the city in order to study, given the dearth of schools near, or in my town that would allow me to pursue studies on my chosen career path. I was ridiculed and found myself in situations of discrimination and racism that were hurtful to me at the time.

Yet, by the same token, although it caused me to disavow my identity as an Indigenous woman temporarily, I rekindled this part of me after concluding that experience. I do not regret any of that process. Every time I am able to share it, I do so generously, because that past fortified me, and it is the reason why I'm here now. I present myself proudly as an Indigenous and Maya woman.

One of the reasons I started making music and felt it expressed my resistance was precisely because I saw the many inequalities imposed upon Indigenous people, and specifically directed towards us as Indigenous women. I was acutely aware of the discrimination we confront, and the opportunities we are denied. The destruction of our land, the dispossession by the State or the military of First People's identity and property is the reason why I want to focus my songs on raising awareness and making this situation visible to the public.[17]

Callan Chythlook-Sifsof was the first Indigenous Alaskan on the United States Olympic Team. Her identity has been shaped by the remoteness of Alaska in historical and physical terms. Her life path from the isolated village to the Olympic village and stardom exposes the complex status of being the first Native woman and only woman of color on a US Snowboard Team. Her homegrown interest in the sport contrasts with the background of most of the other competitors who are groomed from a young age and accustomed to the dynamics of power long entrenched in the Olympic sports' world. She describes her coming into awareness about the multifaceted nature of her identity as it is socially-constructed in life (Yupik/Iñupiat culture, snowboarder, Alaskan, lower forty-eighter, queer).

> My name is Callan Chythlook-Sifsof. I come from a small village from the west coast of Alaska, Bristol Bay; a town called Aleknagik. I grew up there; a town comprised of roughly 200–300 people, 500 miles away from Anchorage, only accessible by boat or plane.
>
> I was on the US Snowboard team from 2006 to 2014. I was raised in the town and when I was 13, I moved to a ski resort just outside of Anchorage, and then at 16, I made the US team, travelled the world, and participated in Olympic qualifications. I competed in the 2010 Olympic games.
>
> I am Yupik Eskimo. My grandpa Adam Triplik did not speak English until he was 10, and my great grandparents never spoke it. They died in the 1990s, when I was a baby. I essentially grew up fully in the Yupik culture, rich in Indigenous traditions in North America as well as Canada. In Alaska, the Inuit people tend to be more intact because of the remoteness of the villages. Furthermore, Alaska did not become a state until 1958, so the colonization happened later than in other parts of North America. It left communities of people alone, like grandpa with his age group, who did not speak English until they were grown. I identify mostly as Yupik because of that richness of that culture and my lack of familiarity with the Northern Iñupiat side.
>
> Once I moved out of the village, that distinction between gender expectations was one part of the culture shock. I noticed very distinct roles for women who do this or men that, or the ingrained [Western] culture that women might not participate across the board. There are outsiders' white cultural norms that bleed into, along with western culture, and invade our villages. I saw gender binary of that sort, but I did not think of myself as a "I am a tomboy for hunting." It was really only after I came out about my sexuality that my awareness increased.
>
> Now I identify as queer, gender neutral, but at the same time, I try not to identify with any label, because this is where my heart comes from, and I identify just as Callan.
>
> In terms of economics, I have had distinct, stark stages that have provoked introspection through contrast. Let me speak to the different cultures with which

I identify and form a part of me, so you can grasp the way those cultural tags have shaped my economic outcomes.

I have a deep cultural identity. I cannot choose this cultural identity with the Yupik people, because it's what I grew up around. It is inherent to me. There are other parts that have had an influence as well. For instance, I happened to like to snowboard in the village, yet did not identify with it. I knew nothing about the snowboard "culture." I was the only person I knew in the village who snowboarded other than my brother. There was no culture at that time involved in snowboarding. It was just a hobby. I never identified as a snowboarder because I didn't know of anyone else in my early years in the village. Then once I started snowboarding professionally, and moved to the ski resort outside of Anchorage, through middle school, I definitely ended up assimilating into the snowboard world.

It is really different in Alaska as opposed to here [Salt Lake City] or Park City. It is not quite as much of an industry. I became part of the snowboard industry and culture, and simultaneously was a kid from Alaska, who had no clue about it. I spent middle school just being one of the kids who snowboarded every weekend and day, engaged in our activities and then once I made the US team, it took me a step further. I became specialized as one of the top performers of the sport, and it was no longer a hobby any more. You are a practicing professional. There was a different echelon of people who chose to take it from a hobby onto that special path. There are people from all over the US; one teammate from West Virginia, a place you might not imagine snowboarders are from. You meet people from Michigan and unique swatches of America—all white people. At the Olympic training center, I was the only person of color. There are probably 200 athletes there on any given day. It was pretty crazy to be the only person of color, but it became normalized. It wasn't something I thought of at first.

I compartmentalized every stage and tried to be in the moment, wherever I was. I never thought, "here I am a village kid, and live this type of life" or, "here at ski resort, I live this other life." I never quite identified with any of those stages, except for my Inuit culture. In fact, it is as though I was a tourist in all these stages of life. Once I was competing fulltime, I was dating a woman from the Swiss snowboard team, and spent a lot of time—about 3 years—travelling back and forth to Switzerland and time in Europe with her, and that was yet another part of Callan. I felt like an alien jumping into each of these experiences, though in a good way, perhaps a tourist or more like an observer of the world.[18]

Davina Dah Yi'itihi Smith (Spotted Elk at the time of interview) worked as the coordinator for Title VI for the Salt Lake School District. She participated as Associate Producer for the KUED documentary film *We Shall Remain—The Navajo* and also as a Production Assistant for *The Long Walk: Tears of the Navajo.* She assisted with Location and Script Consultation for the KUED documentary film *Unspoken, America's Native American Boarding Schools.* Raised in the Monument Valley area, she is a member of Diné (Navajo) Tribe. Davina served as Director of Operations for Utah Dine Bikeyah and the Executive Director of SLC Air Protectors. This year, 2022, she is running for public office in the Utah State House of Representatives District #69.

> Growing up, it was through my grandmother that I came to know activism. Though I am no longer on the reservation, I first saw on the reservation what needs to be done to protect myself and family. However, nowadays I see two worlds.
>
> I grew up on the Navajo reservation. I grew up in the hogan. I grew up without electricity. I slept on the dirt. We lived like that; drove on dirt roads. We had to drive miles to get food, clothing, or water. That upbringing in that space was important to me. From that space and experience, I developed a sense of what was happening to my people, the Navajo people, and how we, to this day, call it rural country. We still have no running water, no electricity and continue to drive on dirt roads.
>
> The healthcare system and our education system is still horrendous. The history of the Indian education school system is, by far, one of the most detrimental, historical traumas for our Navajo people, because of the boarding school system. I, too, was in the boarding school system. I did experience abuse there, not only physically and mentally, but also sexual abuse. I still have to gather my strength from my elders. When I look at my grandmother, my mother, my aunts and my parents, who were also part of the boarding school system, I know they experienced the same things as me.
>
> From these experiences, I might have been a person who followed a path of alcoholism or substance abuse or even suicidal tendencies. I don't because who else will be there to advocate? who else would be there to speak about those that don't have rights? Those who aren't able to speak about these traumas that we've experienced.
>
> I look to my grandmother because she was a person, at age thirteen, who was given away. She ended up having twelve kids. She built her own one stone house. She was also physically abused by her husband, yet I look to that as strength. I know what she went through, which gives me strength. I know whatever I endure, whatever I see, whenever I go and I speak or help anywhere, I know I can do something.[19]

Davina says she filmed "with the local tribes of the State of Utah because our history books do not indicate clearly what the tribes are like here in Utah."[20] These movies expose the Native boarding schools, history of displacement, exploitation, abuse, and discrimination. Her sense of identity was piqued early on when she played the role of an extra in a Hollywood film as a native woman.

> I got my start in feature films. I was in "Geronimo." I had a wonderful experience, but at the same time I knew there was something wrong. It was a small part as a Native wife whose husband was being hung. I remember going to the makeup area where they said to me, "Let's dress her up, but let's make her skin a little more reddish, or darker red. Let's spray paint her hair black." And I said, "Why?" "Well, we need you to fit that part of an Apache." I said, "An Apache does not have red skin. They do not have dark skin. In different regions throughout the US, we are all different. We all do not have black hair. We all do not have red skin. And so, please, I'd like to go as who I am."
>
> Well, we compromised. They made my tint a little darker, but they did not spraypaint me. That was my first understanding, revelation really, of how Hollywood has stereotyped Native Americans or American Indians.[21]

The Not-Your-Mascot movement has fought the appropriation of and use of derogatory Native sports mascots on several fronts. A prominent case brought to the courts in this regard was *Blackhorse v. Pro-Football, Inc.*, which sought to revoke trademark protection of the "Washington Redskins." They advocate against the appropriation of Native identity in legal, professional, and social settings.

Donna Loring supported one of the first bills in Maine to eliminate the use of the word "squaw" from public site names. Around the country, various states, including Colorado, Oregon, Washington, and California, have enacted legislation banning the misappropriation of names, symbols and images pertaining to the Native Americans. This anti-mascot activist talks about the deleterious effect of degrading stereotypes of Indigenous Peoples. She elucidates the urgency and significance of identity and activism, and the need for Native women to promote their own self-representation, either by reformulating or eliminating distortions and appropriations.

> Activism has had a bad rap. I struggle with using that term. It is a term constructed by settlers to marginalize people who are trying to challenge oppressive systems. People have referred to me in that way at moments. I would say I don't have time to challenge these terms.
>
> I like to identify with the notion of being an advocate for my people. Activism or advocacy—my work is definitely rooted in challenging colonial structures. Identifying oppressive systems and structures, confronting and dismantling them. Sometimes we can replace them; however, other times there is no substitute

to an Indigenous-defined solution. In other cases, you just completely dismantle the problem.

That is what we are doing with the Washington team. We are not trying to replace our word, rather eliminate it completely from that context. When it is gone, people can choose whatever name they want as long as it is not Native-themed or Native-based. It is really about dismantling these systems that are designed to subjugate us, keep us in categories, boxes so harmful and oppressive to Native people that define who we are, even though we do not see that image as defining us.

However, the images and symbols do define us on a national level. People look at these images and think that is what we look like. We know that it is not the way we refer to ourselves. Regardless of what we say or do, these systems of power define us, and are the baseline of our identity.

The mascot issue, with regard to the Washington team's name change, is a symbol of how far we have come. We have begun to achieve the humanization of the Indigenous people, and once the name change occurs, we will emerge into a different time frame of how we are viewed on a larger level. It is a symbolic shift with regard to the Native people. We are so much a people identified as a "dying culture, a people of the past, old people."

Now people call us modern Indians, whereas I ask, "were we old? Why refer to us in that manner?" We do not say the "modern Caucasian" or the "modern" … we are people first and foremost. We struggle to prove that.[22]

One staff member for a Native American non-profit dedicated to raising awareness and support for Native environmental issues and financial and political resources for survivable, sustainable communities described her identity as a front-line activist. She reflects:

Many people think of the term activism/movement work as a way of laying claim to yourself. They think in terms of titles, a titleship, or as an ownership of personhood; not really activism as a verb. Activism is action you commit yourself to. For me, activism and activists are the folks that are recognizing the past given to them, carved and forged by the people who came before us. We are doing this work for the people who come after us. Many folks who call themselves activists may not be committed to the entirety of this work or ownership of that title. I like to say I am a human being, who does the work that needs to be done for future generations.

I characterize my work as a facet of my indigeneity. Indigenous people are born connected to the land, and we are reminded constantly that we are of this land, and because of this land we are allowed to exist. My brand of movement work entails reconnecting to the earth and helping people reconnect to their origins.

> Remembering that it's not just one person's story, rather the story of the collective millions who have come before us and will hopefully come afterwards, if what we do now, makes an impact. It will have a lasting effect for more protectors and defenders of the land to come and give way to new life. There will be defenders and fighters, regardless of what day or year it is in America. Everyone has the ability to rise up and fight back, in whatever capacity they have.[23]

Identity is a factor in the commitment to rebuild the communitary way of life, which includes Indigenous values, principles, tangible and intangible cultural practices, and epistemologies. In reaffirming ancestral legacy, identity is part of a continuum and reclaiming of a colonized birthright. Lucia Xiloj explains:

> I seek to reclaim my heritage. Several principles that our grandparents taught us, such as complementarity and duality (in which both men and women are important) need to be part of the process. But this Indigenous communitary [*comunidad*] perception was destroyed during the Civil War and also during the invasion.
>
> We are in a process of reconstructing this Indigenous communitary ideal in which both women and men are truly important, because currently women, especially Indigenous women, have little access to education and health. The only priority they have in life is to marry and have children, which is primarily due to the destruction of this Indigenous communitary concept.
>
> It is important to reconstruct the juridical processes and psychosocial support to continue that Indigenous communitary form of living. These women have a position in society which allows them to be mothers or housewives, but they should also be subjects of law with other options in life.
>
> These are complex processes, because not only do they imply working directly with women to help them become stronger emotionally and psychosocially, but also working with their families and communities as a whole.[24]

The decolonization practices advocated for by these women include a forward-thinking model of asserting a Good Life principle that cherishes nature, humans, and animals over money, power, and accumulation. Many view their activism as innate to their identity, but affirm it as an alternative paradigm for all people and lands.

> I am a Maya Kaqchikel woman, that is my primary identity, with a commitment to struggle. That is to say, I seek change not only for women, but also for People and Nations, in this case, the Maya People of Guatemala, who strive to put into practice autonomy and self-determination. We also aim to reinstate and reclaim the concept of "*Buen Vivir* – Good Life" as a paradigm, which in the West has been considered an alternative to save humanity. It is a new paradigm

> for Westerners, however for us, as Ancient Pueblos, it is a millennial paradigm. It is the basis and sustenance of the Maya civilization.[25]

Simultaneously, as they depict identity, the women draw attention to the universal human plight, challenges faced by more than individual interests and needs. The local is infused with a profound connection to humanity, nature, and the universal. As De la Torre Amaguaña says, "I am committed to the human principles of justice and equality. Some would call it leftist, socialism, Indianism, indigeneity, with a politics of *Sumak Kawsay* [Good Life], where labels do not matter, rather grasping consciousness of the need to be vigilant about the most pressing social issues. We must be committed to the notion that we all share rights as human beings. We all fight for freedom and social justice."[26]

Activism for these women expands its goals to advance the well-being of other native and non-native peoples. They often see themselves as part of the global network, and although they may not all hail from villages or metropolitan centers, they are committed to change work for all. They try to understand Indigenous struggles in their own country, which may implicate various communities (the Latin American designation for tribe) or tribes in the United States. The goal is to connect diverse challenges in order to find the common ground of those who claim Indigenous identity.[27]

Recent attention to the plight of missing native women in Canada and the United States, many of whom most likely were victims of sexual violence as well as disappearance, finds resonance in the cases of sexual violence during the Guatemalan Civil War. Legal work transforms into a form of advocacy to defend women's rights, Indigenous People's rights, and also the inherent rights of nature, as consecrated in Guatemala's constitution. Liliana Hernández describes her attitude toward her profession in this context.

> I am an Indigenous woman and a lawyer, and the first woman to graduate from a university in both my maternal and paternal family. That makes me feel very honored, and it is a greater duty to use the profession that I studied in service of my community and the Indigenous people of Guatemala. I fight for justice, for the collective rights of the Indigenous people. With my testimony of life and struggle, other women feel motivated and inspired to move forward, to change those traditional gender roles which state that they should only be at home making food and taking care of children.
>
> I do that as well, but I also have a profession. I project myself onto my community and on all of the Guatemalan population in the struggle for rights. I am a woman of struggle. A socially-committed lawyer, which means a lawyer that is

not simply in their office waiting for clients, but one that fights for the fulfillment of the rights of Indigenous women and Indigenous communities, especially in the defense of natural resources.[28]

Cristina Marin, Mapuche from Argentina, grounds her defense of women's rights and nature in her ancestor's concepts of Natural Law.

The topic of global economics impacts us heavily, given that many of us are the heads of households, providers, and even more since many of our men do not have easy access to employment. Many of their jobs are temporary … We … engage in more militant forms of public protest for education and health policy, reform, and equity, though that stems from voluntary interventions.

Implicit in that challenge are the structural and soft non-economic barriers of a capitalist country where it is daunting to impose or institute the transformation of consciousness toward respect and protection of biodiversity or *Itrofilmongen* [natural law]. Biodiversity is related culturally and spiritually for us to everything that surrounds us—environment, animals, and people.[29]

As part of the understanding of the nexus between us all, interviewees express an acute awareness of how Western society, politics, colonization, patriarchy, and socio-economics are key determinants of status and identity. They examine how those forces have shaped the identity of Indigenous women and human beings. Many point out the distinctions that arise in the delineation of gender and corresponding roles. Likewise, the pull and centrality of Native epistemologies is not ignored, rather, deliberately embraced as an affirming base for being and living well.

Some of these women explore the intersection of indigenous identity, western constructs of gender, and socioeconomics. Aura Cumes explains:

Regarding gender, I do not assume an identity as a woman. It seems to me that being a woman and being Mayan is a very complicated relationship, because in terms of everyday life and experience being a woman and being Mayan cannot be separated.

Another term which some *compañeras* use is "poor," and these are three links of the chain, in terms of a political struggle. I do not consider myself to be poor. I am not rich either, but the term "poverty," which has a connotation of "misery" in other countries, has been a huge judgment thrust upon the Indigenous people. It is a term which puts us in a place of being subjects who are lacking, but we are not.

Since the processes of colonization, a mechanism of constant pillaging of riches has been imposed on the Mayan people (as with other peoples of Latin America). Their riches have been embezzled in every sense—their spiritual and material riches, as well as their culture. It is a despoiling, which has not stopped them from taking everything from the people, precisely because of the resistance that there has been against it. It is a pillaging that continues and that rears its head again in every moment of history.

I do not consider myself to be poor, but of course in the colonial political economy we are labeled as poor, and are treated as such. It is like being "Indigenous," because before this term was invented in the colonial era we were not Indigenous.

Being a woman is also a matter of dispute because it is another term that has been constructed. These two terms, along with being poor, are the three characteristics that will give form to the struggle, because that is where they situate us. Therefore, what I claim for myself is my identification as a Maya. I do not claim myself as a woman like feminism does.[30]

Luz Maria says:

Based on the general parameters that measure social classification by income, occupation, and education, I can consider myself as middle class. Nonetheless, I should point out that I was born into a humble, uneducated, and illiterate family considered poor by most socio-economic standards because we had no reliable assurance of work and no education either.

I feel I was happy living in a milieu that did not depend heavily on fatuous material wealth. I was not privy to intellectual spaces. I inherited formidable values which have allowed me to love my culture, and to grow up with a treasury of a wealth that today constitutes my social, cultural, and knowledge capital as much as my moral reserves that fortify me to endure the situations in which we live.

The current moment in geopolitics is very complex, since it stems from systems that constantly exhibit inefficiency and inadequacy for tackling our life challenges. The only things that seem to be perpetuated and thriving tends to (re) generate natural, social, cultural, economic, spiritual, and human catastrophes.[31]

And Crystal Tulley-Cordova avows:

As far as gender, I am a Dine Asdzáá. The simplified, less meaningful English translation would be a Navajo Woman. Being such, I have a lot on my shoulders. From growing up in the traditional cultural sense, being the woman in the family is not only the strength, but you're the backbone for the family. You're the one that keeps everyone together. You look out for those that need help.

And you're not only about helping your family, but helping the community. There's a lot of responsibility in this regard from where I come. I recognize that responsibility and realize that my destiny of where I need to go with my career is not for personal gain, but for more of a communal gain and how I can help a larger community.[32]

Most begin their self-representation with a deliberate positioning in the land and dwellings of their ancestral heritage. The tie to a sense of place[33] and belonging to a geographic locale is a recurring trope. Identity is grounded in the particular cultural setting of their ancestral lands. Place is linked to tribal ancestry or clan and a longstanding matrilineage, as in the following examples.

I am Aura Cumes. I am a part of the Maya Kaqchikel people. Kaqchikel is a millenary term- it is one that has survived the processes of colonization.[34]

I am Sharon Asetoyer, who is the daughter of Virginia Asetoyer, who is the daughter of … who is the son of Asetoyer. I am Comanche and welcome. This land is our land. Welcome.[35]

First my tribe. I am Navajo Diné- a citizen of the Diné nation. I am from the Salt clan, born for the Táchii'nii Red Streaking into the Water clan. My third clan from my maternal grandfather, Tsi'naajinii Black Streak Forest People, and my paternal grandfather was from the Salt Clan. I am from Big Mountain, Kayenta Arizona.[36]

My name is Davina Spotted Elk [at time of interview]: Davina Smith is my maiden name. I identify as a Dine' woman, which is Navajo, as we are known. I'm also identified by my Clan system, which in my language is Tachii'nii Tabaaha, as a female, a Dine' woman. Politics? No. If I were in the white man's world, that would be different. But where I come from in my culture, I identify myself as a woman who is head of household, who provides for my children. Being the eldest of my siblings, I'm also the provider for my parents as well because now they are at elder status. We take our clan system from our mothers. We look to our elders. Our grandmothers. We know at some point in our life we will be identified as an elder so we have that close connection to our grandmothers. We watch how they present themselves. How they promote balance and harmony and also protection in the land. Of course, the most important is our connection to Mother Earth, so that's where we gather our strength, with conviction and advocacy. I learned from my grandmother [Katherine Smith], who had always defended her land, where she was born, during that moment back in the 1970s when she was practically forced to relocate from her homeland [Big Mountain]. It terrified me. I learned from her what she did to protect her area, her land, protect where her umbilical cord was buried.[37]

Our [Mapuche] culture is matriarchal. Because of that matriarchy, and in support of them, I [Cristina Marin] work in the field of gender studies integrating the perspective of First Peoples. In that capacity, I am actively involved in the annual national meetings and forums that discuss the rights of Native women in Argentina.[38]

Some of these women are vocal about the inherent relationship between identity, place, and modern sovereignty campaigns.

I, Cristina Marin, recognize myself as member of Mapuche Pueblo, in the territory of Wal Mapu, that is to say the land of the east, also Puelche. Mapuche means *People of the Land*, our cultural identity is Kimún. Our territory is Wajmapu and our language is Mapuzungun. I am a Werken [Spokesperson] for the community. I consider myself first and foremost a militant social Mapuche Tehuelche [Mapuche word meaning fierce people]. Therefore, I insist on the recognition of our People's preexistence and legal right to our territory … What is our intercultural modality in regard to activism? In the state or condition of participation, we are true and genuine to our communities and the organizations constituting them which then spills over into our conception of education. We want to live and learn as First Peoples. Activism is part of our daily struggle. We want to speak and honor our original oral language: Mapudungin, its spiritual elements and the art we produce … Implicit in that challenge are the structural and soft non-economic barriers of a capitalist country where it is daunting to institute the transformation of consciousness toward respect and protection of biodiversity or *Itrofilmongen* [natural law]. Biodiversity is related culturally and spiritually for us to everything that surrounds us- environment, animals, and people.[39]

Whether from the Mesoamerican, Andean, Amazonian, or North American region, the women point to a millenary place of origin and clan, where in some cases, as Davina Dah Yi'itihi Smith says, their umbilical cord, figuratively and literally, has been buried.

At the time of birth, our mothers will hold on to our umbilical cord and then they bury that umbilical cord in a place of significance. For me, mine was buried at my grandmother's home land. What that represents is a link to that home, to that area. Whenever I need rejuvenation or a place to gather myself, I know that is a place. This connects our female grandmothers. For me, it helps me identify what I need to do as a woman, a Dine' woman, in how I behave and, how I think.[40]

Superimposed over place and clan are attributes of an identity delineated by the colonizer and power relations. The women differentiate themselves from socially-constructed imperialist determinations of what gender, socio-economic standards, educational achievement, and knowledge systems should look like. These personal histories and intertwined cultural values contrast sharply from Western colonial models. The women evince an acute self-awareness of who they are today, their relationship with past tradition and lineage, the clash of Western and Native values and determinations of worth, and emphasize their calling to discharge a duty for the preservation and promulgation of their People and territory.

Decisively, the representation of identity begins with the all-powerful act of naming—"I am"—articulating for themselves, as Rigoberta Menchú, Che-Na-Wah Weitch-ah-Wah, Annie Wauneka, and other intrepid Native women had enunciated in order to claim their presence in contemporary history. Some have lived between worlds, on and off the reservation.

> I am Jicarilla Apache and Laguna Pueblo woman, born near and raised in Dulce, New Mexico by my grandmother. I moved and lived 13 years off and on in the Twin Cities with my Anishinaabe, Lakota, Dakota, and Nakota family. I use "she, her, hers" as preferred pronouns. I am a queer, two-spirit, pansexual woman, and do not lay claim to any political party. I am a human being, and a protector of the earth and the land I inherited from my foremothers and ancestors.[41]

It is in the process of naming one's self, and further identifying the enemy, these women are emboldened to assert their subjectivity and eradicate racism. Elizabeth Archuleta explains, "Indigenous feminist theory also presents strategies that empower, which includes naming the enemy, 'reinventing the enemy's language,' and writing to survive."[42] Many Indigenous feminist thinkers begin with the individual "I am" that shifts into the collective "We are" while simultaneously recognizing what they are "not" in their theorization.

Activism

Although many of the excerpts in the previous section stress the intimate relationship of identity and change work, the second topic in these interviews delved into the characterization of activism. How do you define activism? Is activism possible in today's world? Where are the most promising sites of resistance? Appreciating these women's urgent commitment to change involves the historical context of the concept of nation-state, as one interviewee explains.

> We started to expropriate our lands from the multinational corporations that had been supported by the Guatemalan state. Lately, our territories have fallen into the hands of these corporations. The most difficult part is that not only do they control the lands, but they are destroying the territory through their extraction projects, like mining, hydroelectric, monoculture, and petroleum. There are a huge number of large companies that are entering our territories and removing, absconding with everything of value, our riches, from Mother Earth.
>
> Moreover, they have triggered the outbreak of a series of diseases in our people. They have fomented social unrest, and these conflicts are what have caused a divide in our tribal communities and families. There are those in favor of the companies, because the tribal community members are bought. I refer to heads of families, community leaders, and this causes complex clashes amongst us.
>
> Thus, from this example, it is clear, we are permanently implicated in activism. There are protests at the national level as well in each regional level, in every linguistic community. Sometimes there are protests against the very real and dire circumstances in which these very communities are living. This has to do with the capitalist paradigm as well. There is a colonial economic model of extraction and accumulation, which does not allow us any other alternative other than confrontation in this manner because we [Indigenous people] are not participants or beneficiaries, nor are we consulted or meaningfully involved in any part of those projects.
>
> In Guatemala, and other countries of Latin America in the world, ILO Convention 169 from the International Organization of Labor, which in theory and mandate should require consultation with the nation-states before initiating projects of any kind, be they economic, political, or administrative. It all goes unheeded. Consultation and coordination are not undertaken. In addition, the consultation we have conducted in our own communities, and our organizations, the State refuses to recognize.
>
> They do not acknowledge the link and role that these Indigenous consultations play. Neither still, do we seek to have the State alone conduct its consultation prior to the concession of our territories. These are the real and daunting challenges we must face and fight. In that sense, women like us, who confront repressive authorities as in the case of police, anti-protest squads, the very army, and also challenge real troubling examples, like recently in San Juan Sacatepéquez, where sisters were incarcerated, or orders for the capture in Ixtahuacan against the Indigenous. There are various people who have been confronting these forces and actions, like the sisters of La Puya in San Rafael Las Flores. Of the numerous

communities that have been affected, many are the women who have resisted for months, even years against that invasion in our territories.[43]

The commitment to individual well-being and collective *Buen Vivir* is fortified by an Indigenous heritage that fuses resiliency, fortitude, and solidarity in spite of pervasive oppressive histories. Responses describe the undertaking of activism within realms of expertise and training, and not necessarily along a stereotypical model of protest. They weave a patchwork of approaches to making change and advocating for generative solutions in education, athletic competition, theatrical performance, law, environmental justice, and more. Their incursions run the gamut of quotidian resistance from calling out microaggressions to challenging structural racism and violence against Native Peoples on a larger scale. What stands out is a theorization of activism, from a personal, woman-centered, and communitary perspective. The women describe what resistance means and how they are involved in activism that is not the traditional militant protest of the past.

Some people think activism has to be radical or that it has to be loud or visible. A lot of the activist work I have seen of late has been very quiet and subdued, in silent walks, or kids simply making art in their neighborhoods. The youth I work with right now are putting together exhibits without any real coverage because they feel it is something they have to do. There is so much people can do in terms of creative resistance through various forms of art, music, and poetry.

I was in Canada last week and an artist/activist wrote a poem about *Canada 150* and the on-going genocide against Indigenous peoples in a country that's seen as progressive. There are so many ways people are resisting that do not look like what our elders did, or resemble what our adversaries think that it should be, according to their preconceived notions (like setting things on fire or looting).

Many of us are here resisting in new ways. We are tired of fighting, and our means are changing. As we progress into the coming years, with the Trump administration and the fossil-fuels industry that we can't seem to let go of, I feel we will see more and more activism that doesn't look like anything seen before.[44]

Sara Curruchich proclaims:

One of the reasons I started making music and felt it expressed my resistance was precisely because I saw the many inequalities imposed upon Indigenous people, and specifically directed towards us as Indigenous women. I was acutely aware of the discrimination we confront, and the opportunities we are denied.

The destruction of our land, the dispossession by the State or the Military of First People's identity and property is the reason why I want to focus my songs on raising awareness and making this situation visible to the public. I do believe that somehow this is a type of activism, primarily because I do not want to continue complicit in the conventional pattern of musical composition and performance. I refuse to sing only about love, about couples, or anything cliché.

My songs reflect a desire to sing about the contact that the Native people have with the earth, with the air, with the wind. Somehow, even though the colonizer desired desperately to oppress us and sought to steal our possessions, even to deny us that fundamental connection with the earth, I want to express in my music the essential condition we feel that unifies us, binds us to, and with, the whole universe. In some way, it is also through music and the collective nature of that experience, I would like to contribute with the recovery and vindication of the identity of Native people, of our language, and also contribute to the eradication of discrimination and racism.

There are many people in Guatemala who are trying not to remain quiet, and carrying on in a peaceful, non-violent way, showing and saying things as they truly are. That resistance is to some degree like a slap in the face to the entire system that continues to want to oppress and repress us, and does so through violence and aggression. I have met several people who believe they can begin to clear a path for the next generations, a path with transparency, with justice. I know people who sing. I have friends and colleagues who write songs, who paint or dance, or who do theater; each striving to create alternative, peaceful types of activism. The system wants to take that form of expression and resistance away, but fortunately, without success.

Therefore, you see there is a way to continue doing activism. The most important thing is always to stay the course and persist in this activity. Because we are not the same as those military groups, or all those powers that have always wanted to repress our people. If they give us bullets, we give them songs. We give them poems, and that non-violent approach is one of the greatest ways in which we can raise awareness, and in which we can contribute to the structural changes needed in our country.

An artist friend once told me an anecdote about a military group that wanted to kill Sandinista artists, many of whom were male and female community leaders. Someone else told him no, don't fear artists, rather take care of them, because artists carry messages in a very peaceful, yet significant way. Their way can contribute to change. And thus, here we are, many people trying to contribute through their art. Even though the State tries to silence them, there is a very big resistance movement.[45]

Aura Cumes makes the distinction between activism and resistance. She also expresses difference with Mexican *campesina* and other Guatemalan Indigenous activists:

> You can go to the market and come across women who are proudly Indigenous and who have never been part of an organization that stipulates the patterns to follow in order to be a defender of the Indigenous. Resistance exists everywhere.
>
> One of the differences between the Indigenous women of Mexico and us, the Maya of Guatemala, is that we have structured a sense of being Maya without necessarily being *campesinas*. This does not mean that we are degrading the *campesinas*, but rather that we cannot assume an identity as *campesinas* when we have never had a single tract of land to work—we inhabit urban areas. My parents planted for a time, but it did not last long. There are many women who are merchants in the markets that cannot call themselves *campesinas*, since they have made a living in a different way.
>
> I say this because when I was living in Mexico they always assumed I was a *campesina*. When I publish my articles people write comments such as "yes, another *campesina* woman and her struggles," but I cannot usurp a position that is not mine. I am not a *campesina*, because I have never lived that way.
>
> On the other hand, many other *compañeras*, my colleagues that have the honor of being *campesinas* can claim it. The important point is that in Guatemala being Indigenous is not the same as being a *campesina*. This constitutes a more autonomous identity of being Indigenous, unlike other countries, even Mexico, where the more educated you are, the fewer ethnic markers you carry, in anthropological terms. There everything Indigenous is generally associated with *campesino*. So here in Guatemala, being Indigenous has a distinctive feature which is more autonomous in terms of the construction of the self, and the direction of the struggle.
>
> Is it possible to be an activist and fight against everything that is happening? Being a political activist, questioning the system in an organized or disorganized manner is something very different from resisting, because questioning the system is a decision that one makes with the real consequences that attend that decision.
>
> On the other hand, resisting can be done in many ways without even having to raise your voice. There are many silent, unseen resistances that are effective at change of many things. More so than the kind of resistance where one speaks aloud and cries out. There are many people, like my own mother, that say "never go to protests, never react." She (like many other women) has a way of indirectly questioning the system. However, she, more than my father, is the one who has taught me to be proudly Maya with her silent form of resistance.

> There are many people who, due to how sinister this country can be towards people who openly protest, do not openly engage in activism, because open activism is a decision that one makes along with the accompanying risks. Many women are not openly activists who nevertheless have made changes from their place in society, in the ways they are able to do it.
>
> All activism and resistance has as a result not necessarily to always question the system, but rather support it. There are many Indigenous people that consider themselves proudly Indigenous, for example here where I live in Chimaltenango. With their pride and their clothing, they are on the side of powerful groups in this country. They are the Indigenous people that satisfy the quota of multiculturality in those spaces. Being Maya is not a guarantee of always questioning the place of the Mayas, especially for those groups that have economic power due to their position as long-standing merchants. These are the contradictions of the present situation.[46]

For others, activism is a family or ancestral legacy, as Crystal Tulley-Cordova contends.

> Activism. It was a term I was familiar with growing up as a young child. I can remember my father, who has been an environmental activist for a long time, introducing me to the word. Not in the sense of semantic definition, but by acting. By doing so, I do recognize the definition of the word, but not only that, I recognize the responsibilities that come with that word. I identify with the word and the definition because of what I've seen as far as people I'm familiar with who have done activism.
>
> In my research, I talk about an issue that is important to others and explain how that issue impacts others. For example, water not only impacts humans and their drinking consumption, but it can impact the growth of microorganisms. It can impact the growth of vegetation for wildlife.
>
> In these ways, informing people of climatological patterns related to precipitation is a way to be able to be an activist for water. I can say how important it is and how much of a limited resource water is. It isn't a resource with unlimited supply. We need to be environmental stewards of water in a way that is equitable for all living beings, humans, animals, fish, insects, vegetation, etc. Beyond people, since I come from a Native American background, we think of everything as living. Though the bushes and trees outside can't verbally speak to us, we can become advocates for them. They need water as well. The microorganisms that may sometimes be pesky to us depend on it, too. At springs, throughout the Southwest, there is life that's reliant upon the water that comes from springs. In return, that whole cycle for sustainability of life in different areas throughout the world cherishes water.

My work focuses on the Navajo Nation, and from that background I am interested to see how water impacts different parts of life.[47]

Several interviewees quantify in real terms the effect of the structural racism on their change work. Victoria Tubin explains:

I characterize my activism as a leadership of resistance, because we are not living in a framework of logic that disputes discrete moments, rather it is that resistance of saying out loud "we are First Peoples, and a part of humanity, with all of the corresponding human rights. We have individual rights, so why then do you not permit us to live according to the rights inscribed in the UN Declaration of the Rights of Indigenous Peoples? Why don't you make that document effective and apply those standards and principles for the Indigenous people, and women? Why do you reject the premise of those documents by obviously negating our rights to participation and existence in the modern world of the global era?"

I say world because this refers to places far beyond these borders. Here in Guatemala, the First Peoples are discounted, overlooked and neglected—considered worthless. Racism, violence, and everything we experience is quotidian and determinants of our lives.

Taken from their point of departure, the actions of the government, reflected in the national budget provide less than one Quetzal investment in education and health of Maya youth, whereas the *Latina* or *mestiza* receives the benefit of four to six Quetzales per child.

This is where the gross differences in the apportionment of funds for the Indigenous, the uneven guarantee of equal rights, and abominable disparities in freedom and protection of rights for First Peoples in Guatemala becomes evident. We do not benefit from the established laws and rights nor enjoy the same level as everyone else. For these reasons, I consider myself a woman of resistance, part of my grandparents' and ancestor's struggle for freedom.[48]

Activism seeks justice and restitution of lands from which these women's people were historically displaced during colonization. "They are lands that are administered communally, but which lack legal security because the nation has failed to give them title to their property," says Lucia Xiloj. And much of the activism centers on ending the gross, unchecked exploitation of natural resources on their homelands.

I do work with defenders of human rights who are activists, such as the women and men who are engaged in the defense of land against projects, such as mining and the installation of hydroelectric plants, that have been imposed on our

> territory without prior consultation. Above all, I help communities in the legal realm to make visible the violation of their rights as Indigenous communities and as people.[49]

Crystal Tulley-Cordova expresses the beauty and strength of the activism participated in by all of these women.

> I am optimistic in the sense that I can only control myself. I can be the change that I wish to see in the world by making decisions in my life, which I hope are for the betterment of the world. Based on the type of teachings that I grew up with, it's not only that we think about ourselves and our present state of being. I have to think in the same way my ancestors thought before I was here, or before you were here.
>
> They knew that they would have descendants, they knew I would be here. In that sense, I have that responsibility to think about those who have yet to be born. I see that responsibility as change that brings optimism. As an Indigenous person, I have to think of generations beyond myself. There are a lot of people that don't have that frame of mind. If we all engaged in an active movement taking into consideration seven generations beyond ourselves, including all living organisms, we would be in a better state of being.
>
> I see that as my responsibility, to make a ripple in the water where I can. To throw a stone in a big ocean. That's a little harder to see the ripple, but if I threw a pebble in a small pond, I am able to make change within. This is the more optimistic side for me, because it is a change that I am able to make an impact on, especially if there's a community that would be familiar with me and willing to work to be a part of a team to create change.[50]

Notes

1 Interview with journalist, discussion with author in confidentiality, name withheld by mutual agreement, November 11, 2016.
2 De la Torre Amaguaña, in discussion with the author, December 5, 2017.
3 De la Torre Amaguaña, discussion.
4 Tulley-Cordova, *Spatiotemporal examination of precipitation and associated waters in Arizona, New Mexico, and Utah.*
5 Tulley-Cordova, in discussion with the author, October 18, 2017.
6 Benito, in discussion with the author, September 29, 2017.
7 Xiloj, in discussion with the author, September 24, 2017.
8 Cumes, in discussion with the author, September 25, 2017.
9 Cumes, discussion.

10 Batzibal, *Indigenous Women and Education* and *Ancestral Justice*, 194–197.
11 Betasamosake Simpson interview by Abaki Beck, 2017.
12 Interview with activist, discussion with author in confidentiality, name withheld by mutual agreement, September 26, 2017.
13 Tubin, Ser mujer y ser maya.
14 Tubin, in discussion with the author, September 29, 2017.
15 Curruchich, Tejiendo Palabras – Instagram.
16 Curruchich, Videoclip Oficial – RALK'WAL ULEW – Hijas e Hijos de la Tierra – Sara Curruchich – YouTube.
17 Curruchich, in discussion with the author, October, 2017.
18 Chythlook-Sifsof, in discussion with the author, October 2017.
19 Smith, in discussion with the author, October 2017.
20 Smith, discussion.
21 Smith, discussion.
22 Interview with activist, discussion with author in confidentiality, name withheld by mutual agreement, December 11, 2017.
23 Interview with activist, discussion with author in confidentiality, name withheld by mutual agreement, November 15, 2017.
24 Xiloj, discussion.
25 Interview with activist, discussion with author in confidentiality, name withheld by mutual agreement, September, 2017.
26 De la Torre Amaguaña, in discussion with author, December 5, 2016.
27 Interview with journalist, discussion with author in confidentiality, name withheld by mutual agreement, November 15, 2016.
28 Hernández, in discussion with the author, September 29, 2017.
29 Marin, in discussion with the author, November 21, 2017.
30 Cumes, discussion.
31 De la Torre Amaguaña, discussion.
32 Tulley Cordova, discussion.
33 Kermoal, *Living on the Land*, 10–37.
34 Cumes, discussion.
35 Asetoyer, NOW 2007, 55:01–1:14.
36 Anti-mascot activist, discussion.
37 Smith, discussion.
38 Marin, discussion.
39 Marin, discussion.
40 Smith, discussion.
41 Interview with activist, discussion with author in confidentiality, name withheld by mutual agreement, September, 2017.
42 Archuleta, "I Give You Back," 89.

43 Interview with activist, discussion with author in confidentiality, name withheld by mutual agreement, September, 2017.
44 Interview with activist, discussion with author in confidentiality, name withheld by mutual agreement, November 15, 2017.
45 Curruchich, discussion.
46 Cumes, discussion.
47 Tulley-Cordova, discussion.
48 Tubin, discussion.
49 Xiloj, discussion.
50 Tulley-Cordova, discussion.

3

"The Indian Problem"

In the past few years, a new picture of the Indian is projected. In newspapers, magazines, books etc. This new image has shown the Indian as being equal with non-Indians, if not economically then intellectually. In short, people are realizing the actual worth of Indian culture and of the Indian as an individual. The events of the past few months, however, makes one wonder if the people of Maine view the Maine Indians as peers or as beings much inferior to the non-Indian. On the one hand, they pat the Indian on the back, tell him he's doing fine and should be proud etc. and ask when the next pageant is. On the other, when he gets into trouble with the law, it's another story.

Donna Loring

Assimilation into our society can be expedited by having children attend schools off the reservation at a reasonably early age … [I] recommend that the school on reservation be limited to the first five years so they would have to go off and mingle with others … it is our feeling that the policy of the state should be directed toward a more complete assimilation of our Indian citizens into our society, and that our ultimate goals should be to do away with tribal reservations. This last, would of course be a long-range proposition.

Henry Schoolcraft

> The treatment of American Indians today is no different than it was 100 years ago. It is the greatest holocaust in the history of the world.
>
> Winona LaDuke

European colonizers, in the process of taking possession of territory, labor, and resources from Native American populations, formulated a justification of exploitation later referred to by them as "the Indian Problem." A historical retrospective of the problem as conceived by United States and Latin American national policies and laws, as well as the moral justifications used to dominate the Indigenous, provides background to the ongoing debates today. Questions to be considered when confronting this pervasive historical colonizer approach to Indigenous populations reflect ongoing perceptions: What is this essentializing trope of colonization that depicts the Indian as impediment to progress and national cohesion? How does the official nineteenth-century policy of "divide, conquer and civilize," with its blatant disregard for the right of self-determination, continue to be manifested, challenged, and rejected by Native Peoples? What is the reaction of contemporary Native women to the socio-cultural imaginary of the troublesome, disparaged, dehumanized Native that has been internalized by settler-colonizer and imposed on subjugated Indigenous peoples? How do they reframe the question and dismantle the representation in this century? How do they reshape the quandary to reflect an alternative solution, if any exists?

Historically, public discussion on this subject generally separated the Indigenous from the white population into an us versus them dichotomy. In March 1879, General Nelson Miles published an essay in the *North American Review*, then noted for its writings on contemporary issues, entitled "The Indian Problem," summarizing the 400-year-old quandary faced by two groups, European colonizers and the American Indigenous, for supremacy in North America. Miles wrote:

> The real issue in the question which is now before the American people is whether we shall ever begin again the vacillating and expensive policy that has marred our fair name as a nation and a Christian people, or devise some way of still improving the practical and judicious system by which we can govern a quarter of a million of our population, secure and maintain their loyalty, raise them from the darkness of barbarism to the light of civilization, and put an end forever to these interminable and expensive Indian wars.[1]

Since colonization, the solution to this question or "problem" has been euphemistically referred to as one of an "integration of the Indians more fully into the national life,"[2] that is, pacification at the expense of culture, sovereignty, location/delineation of territories, resources, and economic well-being. The Marshall Trilogy of Supreme Court decisions (1823, 1831, 1832), according to the American Bar Association, "established federal primacy in Indian affairs, excluded state law from Indian country, and recognized tribal governance authority. Moreover, these cases established the place of Indian nations in the American dual sovereign structure that still governs today."[3] Legislation such as the Indian Removal Act (1830), Indian Appropriations Act (1851), and Nelson Act of 1889—which called for Native Americans to remove from one reservation and relocate to another—resulted in displacement, disenfranchisement, servitude, and loss of land for presumably benevolent reasons of safety and protection. The Marshall trilogy decisions and various pieces of legislation, all equally untenable, cemented the status of wardship, as Zitkala Sa explained in "America's Indian Problem": "Wardship is no substitute for American citizenship, therefore we seek his enfranchisement. The many treaties made in good faith with the Indian by our government we would like to see equitably settled. By a constructive program we hope to do away with the 'piecemeal legislation' affecting Indians here and there which has proven an exceedingly expensive and disappointing method."[4] Citizenship was granted in the form of Congressional fiat in 1924, rather than through emancipation, further limiting Natives' leverage to fight the embezzlement of land and funds from treaty disputes.

The "problem" and the enacted solutions for it embodied a justification for social, racial, and economic domination of settler-colonizer over Indigenous tribes. The solutions were presumably aimed at closing the gap between these two groups but much more in a manner advantageous to the advancement of colonizers' interests. The Indigenous still strive today to extricate and liberate themselves from these solutions. But it is difficult to reframe a narrative which centered on, as Martin Luther King called it, "genocide," a "scar of racial hatred that had disfigured…society." King wrote, "From the sixteenth century forward, blood flowed in battles over racial supremacy. We are perhaps the only nation which has tried as a matter of national policy to wipe out its Indigenous population. Moreover, we elevated that tragic experience into a noble crusade. Indeed, even today we have not permitted ourselves to reject or feel remorse for this shameful episode. Our literature, our films, our drama, our folklore all exalt it."[5]

Embedding the terminology and mindset of "problem" as an ideology for governing offered a way to retain control of resources and assets located on Native land. With rising costs and accruing expenditures on unoccupied military posts, as well as the perceived Native American interference with expansion policies such as Manifest Destiny, the Dawes Act of 1887 was one of many designed to deprive tribes of ancestral landownership. State-sanctioned enclosure, isolation, and divestiture grew to be the staple of these discriminatory national racist policies. The State traditionally viewed Native governments as "being liabilities and not assets,"[6] yet conveniently would claim that the fossil-fuel, mineral, or other natural resources on reservations fell under the eminent domain of national property and riches. Today the expropriation of tribal resources continues and the challenges tribes face in order to "overcome this paradigm are great."[7] Fair compensation for colonial extractivism in all its forms as well as the emotional trauma endured by cultural pacification makes remediation and reparation complicated, to put it mildly.

What is at stake in material terms is the resolution of the constitutional debate on the nature of tribal sovereignty, the role of the federal government in regulating Indian Affairs, and the rights and responsibilities of tribal members.[8] Rebecca Adamson wrote, in *The Color of Wealth: The Story Behind the U.S. Racial Wealth Divide*: "The official purpose of the Dawes Act was to encourage tribal members to adopt a sedentary agricultural lifestyle and to force Indians to assimilate into white society. Other unstated purposes were to break up tribal governments, abolish Indian reservations, promote individual ownership of Indian land instead of traditional collective tribal ownership and allow white settlers and private business interests increased access to land and other Native natural assets."[9]

Native Americans continue to seek rectification of coerced land transfers. The deep entrenchment of a profoundly colonial paradigm drives Natives to pursue compensation for the material filching of property and land from all Native Americans and especially from women and children, who, because of their gender or age, were egregiously erased from ownership records. Reparations involve far more than monetary compensation, including return of lands, protection of sacred sites, self-determination, and a wide spectrum of rights within the social construct of sovereignty.

From first contact, the economic and physical domination of Europeans over Indigenous included the psychological, holding Natives at fault as "the problem" by imposing a discourse of shame upon them, referring to them as savages and barbaric. The repercussions of this racism targeted at the American Indian emanate society-wide. Colonization by the Europeans had high material, political, and moral costs for Native Peoples, but also settlers. Ronald Chisom, in *Undoing Racism*, explores the philosophical underpinnings and grim repercussions of a society structured on the basis of race, where conformity to racial roles maintains both "inequitable treatment and pathological relations."[10] These commonplace violations of an oppressed people's humanity lead to the experience of racial hostility, violence, and crime for the privileged *and* subjugated members of society. The process of disempowerment can have negative repercussions for society as a whole, not just the marginalized group. Here, however, we will scrutinize the ramifications for the Native populations primarily.

In the best-case European colonizer's scenario, the Indian was viewed as savage albeit, at least in eighteenth and nineteenth-century literature, noble—meritorious of the patronizing benevolence of trusts and wardship. Yet, Indians were viewed as "an impediment to white progress."[11] Sitkala Sa (Gertrude Bonnin) in her essay, "America's Indian Problem," alluded to the non-citizen status imposed on Natives, as an "inheritance of somebody's [Spanish and English colonists] loot." Natives were pigeonholed by the unwieldy category of being problematic wards but were then soon transformed into what Sitkala Sa called "legal victims," disenfranchised from their "own freedom loving land."[12] In fact, in regards to the "Indian Problem," Indian expert Henry Rowe Schoolcraft, in 1828, said of federal legislation, "Nobody knows really what to do."[13]

Assimilationist policy, for example, drove the establishment of boarding school institutions where the United States government could "kill the Indian; save the man," as Richard H. Pratt said in an 1892 conference speech.[14] In one effort to salvage and civilize souls, teachers would muzzle interned students' mouths shut with tape coated in cayenne pepper as punishment for any Indian who uttered words in their own tongue. The boarding school solution, described in his 1853 recommendation to the Bureau of Indian Affairs by its then Superintendent Schoolcraft, would be designed to provide a second-class education to Indians that would "leave him with a hopeless inability to cope with the 'Great White Father.'"[15] Social success for the Indigenous reflected guiding principles of securing a place in society only in exchange for ceasing to be Indian and sabotaging their own "elevation of the Indian race."[16] Russell Means referred to this cultural genocide as a process of "growing into a red face with a white mind."[17]

In the worst-case Indigenous scenario, European policy meant destitution and devastation. As Donna Loring wrote, "Genocide started with Columbus and was carried out during the next 500 years, through military actions, government policies and even educational curricula. Not only forms of mass murders, mutilations, germ warfare, but through policy that was effected to clear land and take the resources. Policies like the Removal Act of 1830 that resulted in the slaughter of whole towns."[18]

Those who survived were displaced and millions of individuals were reclassified, relocated further West onto resource-poor or depleted areas, confined to being perpetually impoverished as tenants on the reservation, "huddled together in little housing projects, because there is no land that we can support ourselves on."[19] United States federal policy expunged colonizer's accountability through consistent sequestering of inhabitants, a disregard for their rights to consultation, and curtailment of self-determination over ancestral lands, culture, natural resources, legitimate governments, and education.[20]

Parallel wise, in colonial Latin America, the "Indian problem" entailed ways to solidify Indigenous people's lowest status in the colonial social hierarchy, wherein they would serve presumably as subjects on landowner's agricultural tracts, called *encomiendas*, or in mines. In reality, although the Laws of the Indies (*Leyes de las Indias*) mandated fair treatment of natives as subjects, distance allowed landowners to abuse their power and instill a centuries-old system of servitude. Bridging the divide between subject and colonizer required a strategy of assimilation that unofficially might occur as "a fusion through miscegenation" in *mestizaje*.[21]

Ostensibly, assimilationist policy had at its core to secure peace and the safety of both Colonials and Indigenous living side-by-side by protecting capital investments, expropriating resources, and ensuring prosperity and loyalty to the crown in generous land settlement packages for Europeans in the Colonial Spanish American empire. Psychological abuse of the Indigenous was the icing on the cake, ensuring further reduction and incapacitation regarding any notions of resistance, revival, and renaissance. In this way, socio-economic enfranchisement of self-identified Natives became an impossibility. Widespread destitution; isolation; and fragmentation of communal identity, political will, and clout were normalized.

For the Indigenous, the continuous conscious and internalized pressure to repudiate all aspects of one's Native identity reinforced this structure of oppression and submissiveness. Ashis Nandy refers to this internalization of inferiority by the colonized in *The Intimate Enemy: Loss and Recovery of Self Under Colonialism*. He introduces the second form of colonization—psychological—as:

> the one which at least six generations of the Third World have learnt to view as a prerequisite for their liberation. This colonialism colonizes minds in addition to bodies and it releases forces within the colonized societies to alter their cultural

> priorities once for all. In the process, it helps generalize the concept of the modern West from a geographical and temporal entity to a psychological category. The West is now everywhere, within the West and outside; in structures and in minds.[22]

Likewise, Louis Althusser examined ideological indoctrination in society at large. The psychological collusion through interpellation (calling) of the subject by Ideological State Apparatus (ISA), a term Althusser used to describe how we conform to ideological indoctrination and accept it as our own, comes into play in the psychological machinations of colonization. This is not to equate colonization with ideological programming of society, given that the first depends on the use of violence to wield control. Yet, ideology and colonization (the violent imposition of roles) act upon the psyche of both colonizer and colonized. Internal recognition of roles in society is accepted vis-a-vis an understanding of culture's place in relation to power. Unlike the physical brutality implicit in colonization, ISA addresses people (interpellates them) in subtle unconscious ways to construct identity and place in society. For Native Peoples, the intersection of ideological indoctrination and physical violence of colonization imposed a social imaginary difficult, if not impossible, to deconstruct.

Beyond the bureaucratic, political, physical, and emotional manipulation enacted in the name of the State's or Crown's interest and defense, in the religious context "the Indian Problem" framed the Indigenous as heathen creatures requiring Christian redemption and salvation. Natives were considered an unwavering obstruction to the peace and prosperity of the triumvirate of power: the landed elite, the State, and the Church. Proselytizing and attempts to convert Indians imposed a series of valuations and judgments regarding their morality, intelligence, and even of their categorization as human beings. The proposition essentialized the Indigenous in deprecating ways.

The counter-hegemonic Black Legend writings, emerging in the tomes of the sixteenth century, denounced colonial Spanish cruelty and intolerance in their imperial quests, as published historical exposés of the era. The documents disseminated the criticism flagging the inhumane treatment characteristic of colonization practices. Best known of these critics was Bartolomé de las Casas, who, in his famous *Historia de las Indias*,[23] begun in 1527 and completed in 1561 shortly before his death, called for the abolition of Indian slavery and turned colonization from an official history of conquest and triumph into a candid description of the insidious moral treatment of the Natives. This manuscript, however, was not printed until 1875.[24]

Twentieth-century essayists in the Latin American region reevaluated the Indigenous to understand the role of the population in modern nation-states. Some idealized, glorified, and exalted native cultures as alternatives to the alienated modernity of the Western industrial complex. However, beginning with the Realist literary movement that explored national identity formation, literature explicitly propagated the dichotomy between races in the new republics. For instance, Peruvian socialist José Carlos Mariátegui (1894–1930) in "The Problem of the Indian," published in his book *Seven Interpretive Essays on Peruvian Reality*, more than 300 years after colonization, reiterated the flawed historical approaches taken from the perspective of ecclesiastical, moral, socio-economic, racial, administrative, or legal sources.[25] Mariátegui reoriented the understanding of this problem away from moral grounding toward socioeconomics.

> Any treatment of the problem of the Indian—written or verbal—that fails or refuses to recognize it as a socioeconomic problem is but a sterile, theoretical exercise destined to be completely discredited. Good faith is no justification. Almost all such treatments have served merely to mask or distort the reality of the problem. The socialist critic exposes and defines the problem because he looks for its causes in the country's economy and not in its administrative, legal, or ecclesiastic machinery, its racial dualism or pluralism, or its cultural or moral conditions. The problem of the Indian is rooted in the land tenure system of our economy. Any attempt to solve it with administrative or police measures, through education or by a road building program, is superficial and secondary as long as the feudalism of the *gamonales* continues to exist.[26]

Others, like González Prada, analyzed the ramifications and repercussions of either not dealing with or resolving "the problem" of the Indigenous in his essay, titled oddly with the possessive adjective, "Our Indians."[27]

> The problem of the Indian is economic and social more than educational. How is it to be resolved? Not long ago a German conceived the idea of restoring the Inca Empire. … But is there any place for such a restoration today? If it were attempted and carried out the result would be a petty imitation of past greatness.
>
> The situation of the native can improve in two ways. Either the heart of the oppressors relents to the extent of recognizing the rights of the oppressed, or the spirit of the oppressed acquires sufficient vigor to chasten their oppressors. If the Indian were to spend for rifles and bullets what he wastes on alcohol and fiestas, or if he were to conceal a weapon in the corner of his hut or on the hollow of a rock, he might change his situation, making his property and life respected. To violence he might then reply with violence, punishing the patron who steals his

wool, the soldier who levies in the name of the government, and the bandit who robs his cattle and beasts of burden.[28]

Of the colonizer's normalizing trope, used to subjugate and exploit Native people, the women interviewed here addressed how this played out in their experiences. Although still insidious and pernicious, contemporary thinkers deconstruct the circumscription of Native Americans as uncivilized infantile obstacles to progress with rigorous rhetorical and cognitive savoir-faire.

Rebecca Adamson, taking a macroeconomic approach, points out the need to realize the complexity of development and prosperity for different segments of society and geographical spaces of the United States and of Tribal Nations. In "Land Rich, Dirt Poor," she considers the systemic economic failure in US society as analyzed in conjunction with the problematization of Native culture, given the interdependence between broad-scale economic issues and Indigenous circumstances. For her, the question for the Indigenous must be understood in "relationship with the greater [structural] problem, the economy must fix the larger problem in order not to fail. My culture is not the problem and yet, the consciousness that created the Indigenous problem will not be able to solve it."[29] Psychological liberation is the *sine qua non* of anti-colonialism.

For others, the solution comes only as an awareness of the late twentieth-century renaissance of Native resistance and solidarity movements across borders. A speech by Jimmie Durham at Harvard in 1977 on the international implications of the First Peoples' issue catalyzed Winona LaDuke's understanding of the problem as an international indigenous human rights struggle. Globally, Natives began to shift from passive victims under the hold of psychological colonization to joining ranks to determine their own destiny through political work and self-determination efforts. Comprehension grew with the understanding that *world-wide* resource exploitation inflicted human rights violations most pronouncedly on Native lands and people.[30] There was, and still is, a need for profound change in the ubiquitous and illegal policies of this exploitation. LaDuke recalls that Durham's talk, advocating a global perspective of solidarity around these issues, made her feel as if she was "finally making my way home".[31]

A commonly articulated imperative underscores raising consciousness about the dehumanization processes used to manipulate the Indigenous. Structural barriers in the form of bureaucratic agencies buttress abuse and exploitation of the derogatorily labeled "primitive barbarians." For instance, LaDuke points out that Native policy in this country was handled first in 1824 by the Bureau of Indian Affairs, a department within the Department of War, and later under the Department of the Interior. This bureaucratic structure enshrined the idea of "the only human beings [in the world] treated as a natural resource,"[32] a United States idiosyncrasy. The fight to legitimize the Indigenous as people was a charge that had to be taken up in the late twentieth century by the United Nations under international law in its *Declaration on the Rights of Indigenous Peoples,* classifying the Indigenous as people with fundamental rights to self-determination, language, land, territoriality, children, and natural resources.

In her capacity within state government as tribal representative, Donna Loring continually flipped the coin to make visible and bring an insider's view to the face of discrimination and exploitation of First Peoples when it takes place in the name of societal (state and country) good. Though she lost many battles during her tenure in the Maine legislature in defense of the rights and protection of tribal nations, her persistence and savvy allowed for a keener understanding by non-Natives of the history of exploitation and victimization of the tribes.

Another line of action against the normalizing trope is related to the anti-mascot movement supported by the National Congress of American Indians (NCAI). It aims to eliminate the appropriation and commercialization of Native-related words and/or images as derogatory and harmful stereotypes of Native people—including sports mascots. These depictions are rampant in media, sports, and popular culture. Part of the legislation in Maine which Donna Loring sponsored in April 2002 was related to the misappropriation of the word "squaw." 2020 was a watershed year for legislation around the country that enforces removal and a change of names that are derogatory, or an option that could allow some schools to keep using team names, like the Utes at the University of Utah,[33] with consultation and permission from affected tribes. Commandeering of native-related terminology for profit or designation of non-Native owned businesses is another facet of the erasure of Native identity, rights, and material well-being.

In the judicial courts for Trademark Trial and Appeal Board, Patent and Trademark Office jurisdiction, Amanda Blackhorse, Marcus Briggs-Cloud, Philip Gover, Jillian Pappan, and Courtney Tsotigh v. Pro-Football, Inc. sought to cancel respondent's registrations under "Section 2(a), 15 U.S.C. § 1052(a), which prohibits registration of marks that may disparage persons or bring them into contempt or disrepute."[34] Prior to this trademark case, Harjo et al. v. Pro Football, Inc. in their 1992 petition, asked the "U.S. Patent & Trademark Office to cancel the lucrative federal trademark licenses of the dreadful name of the Washington NFL franchise."[35] The most recent decision was overturned by the Supreme Court in 2017. However, the name was finally changed by the owner of the team in 2020, in the wake of the Black Lives Matter protests. The trajectory taken before the courts for recognition and reclamation, on the part of all concerned, was time-consuming, money-consuming, and, particularly for the plaintiffs involved, exhausting.[36]

Several efforts have been made to transform the cultural imaginary in the minds of young people studying in our educational system by mandating curriculum about state-specific and federal Indigenous history and its cultural traditions. These educational initiatives are designed to open young minds to transforming derogatory narratives. As Christine Ayers, a Montana school teacher, said about her Native students: "These kids don't really get a mirror to look at… I think [this instruction] helps both native and non-native kids understand everyone's culture."[37]

For Loring, her fight to pass bills on changing stereotypes, educating about, and protecting Native families and children, brought humility, compassion, and an inside view of what goes through the minds of the colonized during state-sanctioned illegal transactions: "…all I could think of was my ancestors and how pained they must have been to have to beg for their lands and their lives in these very halls and this very chamber [Maine House of Representation]."[38] Her papers, including newspaper clippings and other literature by and about her, reveal her unabashed and bold outspokenness about Native history and the egregious infractions imposed upon the Indigenous since colonization.

The responses and reactions to "the Indian Problem" by contemporary Native women articulate an imperative to move beyond the notion. Many of the interviewees commented on how outdated it is. However, the paradigm remains in force. Uranium extraction and other pervasive environmentally hazardous practices in the name of domestic energy policy or national security continue to go unchecked. During recent gas and oil pipeline expansion and hydraulic fracking which illegally traverse tribal lands, inciting protest and lawsuits, corporations fell back on "the Indian Problem" defense. The reduction of the Indigenous in this manner continues to be relevant as governments protect corporations over the sacred lands. LaDuke, addressing the United Nations Fourth World Conference on women and NGOs in 1995 asserted that decisions are made by corporations with an interest entirely different from that of the land and the people of the land. Corporations seek to increase their money coffers whereas tribal nations set a goal to protect the land and the people who inhabit that affected space. Corporate apathy and federal government negligence concerning both human and natural resources is pervasive. LaDuke refers to this as a "predator/prey relationship" which industrial society has developed with the Earth and the people of the Earth.[39]

Contemporary anti-Native backlash takes many forms, although it shares the rationale outlined in "the Indian Problem" as foundational.[40] Some have called American Indians "social parasites," living the high life on the mistakenly glorified "welfare" bandwagon. The ignorance of racism provides an underhanded vitriolic campaign strategy for laying claim to Native property. However, high poverty rates on many reservations, ever-shrinking lands stolen from treaty agreements, and other quantifiable data bear out the untenable economic situation for Natives. Solutions to Native Peoples' challenges must address short-term needs as well as the long-term impact on the heirs of earlier attempts to reduce "the Indian Problem." Solutions require expunging a system where the Indians "remain tenants on their own land," where "our social health is your economy and health as well," wrote LaDuke, asserting that "your [white] economy, your [white] welfare and your [white] long-term interests won't be better either…" if the current system remains. LaDuke suggests considering these questions when framing a discourse regarding the issue: "Can a person who lives in the north woods of Minnesota have thoughts big enough for national policy debate? Can men of privilege, who do not feel the impact of policies on forests, children, or their ability to breastfeed their children actually have the compassion to make policy which is reflective of others?" [41]

As a Native, as a human being, as a mother, LaDuke understands the issues and questions all—from the government certification of ingredients that allow highly sugared cereal or unhealthy mercury levels in fish consumed by the American public to treaty enforcement.

Elizabeth Archuleta, Native ethnic studies professor, explains why these questions are important: "We believe theory comes not from abstract written ideas but from the collective knowledge of Indigenous women whose lives have not informed feminist theories, methods, or policy concerns and whose lived experiences mainstream feminists will continue to ignore unless Indigenous women question and deconstruct existing methodologies…Indigenous women's work that produces knowledge based on one's lived experience is a form of theorizing."[42]

****

The Bureau of Indian Affairs, in 1853, published a policy recommendation for subduing the "wilder tribes" by Henry Rowe Schoolcraft, who wrote: "…it is indispensably necessary that [Indians] be placated in positions where they can be controlled, and finally compelled, by stern necessity to resort to agricultural labor or starve." Has this position changed over the years?

One might ask oneself how it would feel to be labeled a problem, to have one's sacred spaces turned into recreational parks or drilling sites for oil. If an observatory was built on land that is held sacred, or contained the burial sites of your ancestors, even in the name of national or scientific advancement, would you allow it? How would it feel to know that there was a federal policy designating barriers to your educational attainment and professional growth based on race or ethnicity? Can you imagine being told your people are an impediment to national progress, based on an historical fallacy of "discovery," when prior to that discovery, your ancestors had been the original inhabitants for centuries of the land in which that nation thrives?

In each of these interviews, be it from the perspective of a scientist, sociologist, anthropologist, environmental activist, politician, athlete, singer, legal witness to atrocities, the same reaction prevails. Each of these women proclaim: We stand here, competent, educated and productive, contributing to the well-being of our community and our planet. Is our culture lesser than yours, our knowledge illegitimate and invalid? Is our identity and gender not equal to yours? We are not the problem.

Notes

1 Miles, "The Indian Problem," 304.
2 Clissold, "The Indian Problem in Latin America," 47.
3 Fletcher, "Short History of Indian Law."
4 Zitkala Sa, "America's Indian Problem."
5 King, *Why We Can't Wait*, 89.
6 Loring, *In the Shadow of the Eagle.*
7 Loring, *In the Shadow of the Eagle.*
8 Robles, *The Color of Wealth*, 29–73.
9 Robles, *The Color of Wealth*, 46.
10 Chisom, *Undoing Racism.*
11 Loring, in discussion with the author, 2017.
12 Zitkala Sa, "America's Indian Problem," 185.
13 Limerick, *The Legacy of Conquest*, 195.
14 Pratt, "The Advantages of Mingling Indians With Whites, 46–59, "A great general has said that the only good Indian is a dead one, and that high sanction of his destruction has been an enormous factor in promoting Indian massacres. In a sense, I agree with the sentiment, but only in this: that all the Indian there is in the race should be dead. Kill the Indian in him, and save the man."

15 Schoolcraft, "BIA policy recommendation," 18.
16 Miles, "The Indian Problem," 309.
17 Means, "For the World to Live, Europe Must Die."
18 Loring, Donna M. Loring papers.
19 LaDuke, Winona LaDuke papers, "Editorial."
20 Miles, "The Indian Problem," 313.
21 Clissold, "The Indian Problem," 48.
22 Nandy, *The Intimate Enemy*, 11.
23 Bartolomé Las Casas, del V. F. R. A. Fuensanta, and Rayón J. L. Sancho. *Historia De Las Indias*, Madrid: Imprenta de Miguel Ginesta, 1875.
24 Sale, *Conquest of Paradise*, 345.
25 Mariátegui, "The Problem of the Indian," 22–30.
26 Mariátegui, *Seven Interpretive Essays on Peruvian Reality*, 22–30.
27 Gonzalez Prada, "Nuestros Indios," 311–338.
28 Gonzalez Prada, "Nuestros Indios," 311–338.
29 Adamson, in discussion with the author, 2017.
30 Means, "For the World to Live, Europe Must Die," 31.
31 LaDuke papers, box 1 file 5.
32 LaDuke, Papers, box 1 file 4.
33 Gehrke, "Utes can keep their name," *Daily Utah Chronicle*, September 6, 2005.
34 Blackhorse et al., "Cancellation."
35 Harjo, "Offensive mascots belong in museums and history book."
36 Interview with activist, conducted in confidentiality by the author, name of interviewee withheld by mutual agreement.
37 Klein, "Native American History Is Often Overlooked in Schools."
38 Loring, *In the Shadow of the Eagle*, 63.
39 Berghof, "Environmental activist Winona LaDuke shares a powerful message of hope," 6.
40 Grossman, "Treaty Rights and Responding to Anti Indian Activity."
41 LaDuke papers, "Vice Presidential Campaign Discussion 1996."
42 Archuleta, "I *Give You Back*," 89.

4

Responses to "the Indian Problem"

The interviewee's responses to the European colonizer trope essentializing Native Peoples as "the problem" exemplify a form of "generative refusal"—a rejection of negotiation with colonialism, instead engaging in practices that bring an alternative and better future to self-determination.[1] They recounted their perspective and the effects this nomenclature had and continues to have on their psyche and that of their communities. They described what it feels like to be considered a problem and explored the ways in which they figuratively distance themselves from "problem" in order to dismantle the rhetoric of oppression.

Assuming the Indigenous as a question, or problem, is to reduce people to objects, seen as a burden, and impediment to progress.[2] It objectifies and provides the rationale for genocide, or appropriation of lands and natural resources.

Crystal Tulley-Cordova approaches the issue from her perspective as a geologist.

> Classifying things as an "Indian problem," for me, has a negative connotation right away, especially thinking about the history that Native American people have gone through with westward expansion, putting my ancestors in encampments, taking them away from their tribal homeland: Thinking that the Indians are always a problem.

> I have witnessed that negative connotation of being Indigenous as something that is bad or something seen as "less than." If you're from an Indigenous background or if you're Indian, these negative things are wrapped up in the definition of being Indian. We could think of these as negative stereotypes. Or what people might think of as positive stereotypes of being Indian, like the color of their skin, how they act, or substances that may impact their life. There are all these different things we can think about.
>
> Now, in considering a problem: If you just state, "there's a problem," that tends to have a hierarchal meaning that someone else is saying we're a problem. It really is based upon the definition of who has the power to say the words, which would be equivalent to arbitrarily applying the concept to any other ethnicity. They're a problem as well. This creates an inequality for people in thinking that one is higher than the other by using terms or stating that an ethnicity or a people are the problem when there is an opportunity to see what skill set people have. So, for example, being Native American, what type of skill set do we have?
>
> In my particular case or field, what skill set can I bring as a Native American person to STEM, to science? The type of background I can bring is based on the fact that I have this knowledge and that we're not the dominant creatures on earth. There's a whole cycle of natural being, a natural state out there that we need to take into account. If we mess with one thing, it's going to bring imbalance to another thing. We know this well given the current state of the atmosphere.
>
> With regard to being Native American, we have to inform others that don't follow those types of teachings, and tell them this might be a different way of thinking. That's why I really enjoy the interdisciplinary type of work and research that I do because I can bring those ideas to the research that I do. I've been really successful in the research that I've done. It's a large study area, similar in size to West Virginia, and the four-year duration of my study is also unique. The research methods that I'm using haven't been used before. In our culture, we're taught "Tóeíiínaat'é" meaning "Water is Life." This teaching has been influential in my studies. I dedicated my dissertation "To those who have come before me, who have taught the importance of Tóeíiínaat'é." This is an acknowledgement for my ancestors, people who colonizer's deemed part of the Indian problem.[3]

The moral argument in theological, ecclesiastic terms presumes the white man will be the salvation of the savages, bringing civilization and religion to their unruly ways. From the point of view of social and economic development, white settlers have often dictated and imposed their models of progress and success on the Native population, under the assumption that they can save them from themselves. This inane idea receives much push-back in the interviews.

As an Indigenous educator and one who has been the target of these salves of salvation, Luz Maria de la Torre Amaguaña states:

> People believe "We are going to help the natives;" but we no longer need saviors nor have we ever needed them. Today we must inaugurate that other way of joining together as human beings. The path we are on leads to a lack of unity of the Indigenous peoples of the north and the south, of whole nations, not only Indigenous, but Afros, *mestizos*, whites, and all colors. We need to come together, and be conscious of decolonizing the dominant matrix as we exhort "join us north and south." The feminist movement in the beginning of the struggle fought for rights, but the feminists forgot about the Indigenous. That does not have to happen. The feminist movement has also retreated tremendously, and is now working on the issue of being a woman with differences, heterogeneity, a break-through. Nonetheless, much remains to be done.[4]

Others not only reject the notion of deliverance by the "Great White Father," but also deconstruct the entire discourse of subjugation that conveniently turns the Indigenous into the instigator and responsible party of his/her own miserable condition. Suggesting that we be clear about who initiated and invented this problem, and for what reasons and interests, pedagogue Victoria Tubin counters the logic to introduce epistemological difference.

> There are many aspects to address here. First, when we refer to an Indigenous problem, let us remember who initiated and posed this "question." They are speaking about a different reality and a distinct context. It is an epistemological problem, so how it is addressed in academia, in economic discourse, and the discourse of our government is distinct. When they say the Indigenous problem, it is rather like adding one problem to another. For them it is not structural, and we fundamentally understand this issue posed in distinct ways. When they refer to this problem, it is regarding our clothing, or that we are thinking about land which is not arable or useless. What they do not say is that they need our land for their megaprojects. It is an epistemic problem: those who pose it, how they frame it, and how they hear our demands by those questioning the State.[5]

Turning the question on its head makes implicit the blindness of the modern State—an entity that still does not envision interculturality and diversity as a necessary first step for redressing a divisive and racist approach to societal well-being. Juana Batzibal Tujal explains:

> The crux here is that the Indigenous pueblos do not concur, and we do not see ourselves as the problem. Yet the problem lies within the State that cannot visualize the actual composition of the entire Nation. Neither can, nor does it, understand that the economic model, that is functioning and imposed by them, is flawed, and if they continue to utilize that economic model, then "we are the problem." However, with respect to our own model of development, they are the problem.
>
> The question is how to find a middle ground where we all can be participants in our own development. Beginning with that middle ground of the public sphere, all those in public office have a responsibility to truly see, understand, and represent their specific nation.
>
> Here [Guatemala] those in the government seem not to know the history of their people. They base themselves in the philosophies of those [non-Maya] governing the State. However, we must realize that it is the Maya philosophy, the very principles and values of the Maya cosmovision, that they do not know. For them, the Maya philosophy is a thing of the past. The Maya lived in Tikal or those [Maya] currently alive, who they consider to be ignorant, illiterate, and unable to contribute to development.
>
> Nonetheless, we are the ones responsible for the economic growth of this entire Guatemalan nation. In that sense, we are not the problem. Neither are we an ethnic problem, as Héctor Díaz-Polanco called it. The ethnic question has nothing to do with this subject. We are a pueblo, a community of people, who seek our own development through autonomy and self-determination, which implies a return to, taking up if you will, of the concept of Good Life [*BuenVivir*]. That is the paradigm we are trying to recuperate from the perspective of our ancestors.[6]

The modern nation state, from the Indigenous perspective, is the problem. Multiple resistance movements exist in "the Americas," all of which are creating a network and connections for change work. Various Native proposals are emerging from communities living in adverse conditions who seek to transform modes of living and strengthen a resurgence of their culture.

This is an extended contest. An anti-mascot leader gives this example of the constant barrage of discrimination faced by the Indigenous when it comes to protest efforts.

> We went to a rally last week where the Washington team was playing the Chargers. One man walked by us, a Chargers fan, seeing we had been asking people to stand with us. As he approached, he had his shirt covering his nose, said "you all smell like shit." We had been asking the Washington fans to turn their shirts inside out and join our protest.

> Comments like that bring you back to that issue and the history of Indigenous people here. I know they are ignorant people, who say whatever they want. However, when you get into the mind of average everyday people, that is precisely what it looks like and it turns into armed resistance against us, when we protest.
>
> There was a peaceful group of us, women and children who were marching, about 20 or 30 people. What have we ever done to any of them? We were faced with armed people, standing there protecting what? Property? They told us we had to leave. Were they going to shoot us, protecting that piece of the parking lot? It takes me back to a bad time.[7]

Yet the Indigenous rebut the twisted logic of intentional humiliation. One way to do so is through artivism.

> Remy Johnson does digital work. He is an *artivist*. He uses his art to create images that make people think. The other day he showed me a sticker he made that is called the Indian Problem; the individual is holding a Molotov cocktail, and wears a feather head band. Remy tries to use the negative images to combat this stereotype. They always label us as being a problem, "you people hanging on to this and that."[8]

Artivism is an aesthetic movement in which singers, performers, visual artists, dancers, poets, and others elaborate their creations on sites of contestation in collaborative fashion. Rooted in a late twentieth-century gathering of Chicano artists from East Los Angeles and a key militant Indigenous group in the Chiapas uprisings, the concept is one of alternative resistance particularly focused on decolonization. An intersection of art and activism, its definition, and application, is broad. Rachel Presley states that, "Performing these embodied liminalities as a generative decolonial practice…evocatively reclaims individual identities and opens up space for affirmative communal living."[9] Pieces might be created "in the defense of nature and Indigenous social movement in dialogue with women activists on the front lines of environmental struggle."[10] Artivism has also become a powerful statement regarding the disappearance and murder of Indigenous women.

Understood from sociological and historical perspectives, the contemporary roots of "the Indian Problem" stem from a deep structural racism which continued as the independence movements of Latin American national identity took shape in the twentieth century. Aura Cumes traces the codification of this discrimination as it was systematized in the seats of power.

> The Indigenous problem is a completely racist and colonial term. It was used in Latin America in the 1920s, 1930s, 1940s, and 1950s when the *criollos* held parliaments to ask "what do we do with the Indians?" because the colonial process erased the fact that the Indian is not the problem, but rather the problem is the process of pillaging.
>
> After the colonialization, the structuring of the liberal processes with their idea of progress constructed an impoverished Indigenous person who would be the cause of their own poverty. Therefore, those history-erasing years have caused the term "Indigenous problem" to become naturalized.
>
> The Indigenous problem says that we are the problem because we are incapable of developing, of integrating ourselves, of forgetting our backwardness to be able to aim for progress, development, etc. It is very much a colonial term, and at this point (at least in Guatemala) we do not use it in academic environments, and in fact, we ought to problematize it more forcefully. Here the Indigenous people are not the problem, the problem is the constant pillaging of the Indigenous population that continues to this day.[11]

Antonia Benito acknowledges the historical premise and demonstrates the ongoing resistance of Indigenous Peoples to the fallacy. For centuries, Natives have opposed and discounted the hegemonic logic through their resiliency and cultural cohesion.

> We are essentially Original People from First People's Communities, and historically they have seen us as a problem, but we have been able to demonstrate just the opposite. There are Indigenous professionals in different areas, and there are also Indigenous people who are not professionals that are examples to us as young women. They are people that make changes in the country and develop a way of organizing themselves. They have been an example to us because through them we continue to learn about how to communicate in the communities, as well as the manner in which we can keep our own ways of valuing life, language, communication, organization, and economies vibrant.
>
> We are still alive. I do not believe we are a problem, because if we were, if they still viewed us as they did twenty years ago, we would not exist anymore. But we are strengthening ourselves. I can assure you that in the present time, with women and Indigenous teenagers, the subject of duality in Mayan spirituality is fundamental. Another achievement has been the addition of elderly people to the Network of Indigenous Youth of Latin America, which shows that right now efforts are being coordinated in different spaces.[12]

The contemporary application of the idea that Indigenous People are an obstacle to progress is demystified by Liliana Hernández. She points to national governments and world banking institutions whose financial profit and monetary interests motivate their continued exploitation of Indigenous Peoples. Hernández places responsibility for current biases on these institutions.

> The Indigenous Problem has been a justification on the part of the colonial state to erase our history and, furthermore, to justify the pillaging of all of our cultural elements. Not only the external material aspects of culture, like our fabrics, traditional medicine, architecture and gastronomy, but also the seizing of possessions and resources, such as rivers, mountains and territories.
>
> This term which states that we are a problem currently has a new meaning, because they call us enemies of progress. When the Indigenous people take a stance, when there is resistance against the imposition of extractive projects, they consider us a problem all over again. The World Bank and the financial banks consider us to be a problem, and the government as well, because we are "enemies of development or terrorists that reject progress." Therefore, this term is still used in the present to justify this pillaging.[13]

Sara Curruchich points to the benefits of racist policy for the nation-states as they try to assimilate Indigenous Peoples into the status quo while erasing their cultures. She rebuffs attempts to deny this reality when dismissing Indigenous rights.

> The phrase "Indigenous problem" is an ever-present structural impediment that continues to exist. It stems from deep-rooted discrimination and segregation that our country still exhibits. The ongoing classifications and determinations as to who can access certain things, who will be denied, who can enter some place, and who cannot enter another, are real.
>
> I speak frequently on this topic because this is one of the biggest issues we must address: racism and discrimination towards Indigenous people in general exists. As Indigenous People, we have received comments about "why" we exist, even using contemptuous lexicon for those who are from the "interior" of Guatemala. Some complain, why do we [the Indigenous] have to come to the city to protest or revalorize our institutions? They [city] have no comprehension about how their ignorance affects my village, and moreover in some way, the entire population.
>
> Nonetheless, our exclusion has not diminished. It is a complex, complicated problem because in our society, certain classes hold onto resentment against the Indigenous people and refuse to look beyond the constructed superficial reality. Indigenous people have suffered greatly throughout history; communities have been razed, women raped, women have had fetuses removed forcibly from their wombs. Enormous atrocities have been committed.

> Even today there are those who maintain that all this is an exaggeration. Somehow this blindness stretches for some individuals so far as to suggest that the Indigenous people are the problem. Moreover, there are many who believe that the Maya or Native people of the villages no longer exist, and think that the Maya, for example, only existed thousands of years ago.
>
> Also, another misconception and stereotype is that we claim our identity and self-identify simply to elicit compassion, or request money, or as economic parasites. During the history of Guatemala, specifically from 1960 to 1996, the thirty-six years of the internal civil war, there were many forced disappearances. In some way, the fact that many of the families have not been able to recover the bodies of their loved ones means that there isn't any healing or closure because even today they keep searching, looking for, and seeking information.
>
> Even witnessing this, many people are so blinded. Perhaps it is not their fault, rather Guatemala itself and those in power who deny us the knowledge of our own history. They actually think the families are throwing childlike tantrums when they keep saying, "I want to find my daughter," "I want to find my son," "they took him, I want him back." They still think that it's just an excuse, if you can conceive of this, as a means to justify or to gain some kind of financing or handout.
>
> Why do other people think this? It's because of the mediocre education that we have in Guatemala. During one's childhood, as young girls, we are taught that Guatemalan history is comprised of three ships that came and took away the gold. Then they left, and that's the whole story. They do not tell us how people were massacred. They do not tell us that despite all that, even today there are many people who are still being murdered, who are still being robbed, people from the communities that are still being raped, for example, and who are still criminalized for wanting the same life as others.
>
> We do not know our history. Knowing our history is crucial in order to take those big steps, so that they do not see us, the Indigenous people, as a problem, and in turn we are led to believe we ourselves are a problem.[14]

Some discuss "othering" and the effects and implications that occur in contemporary society when one group is targeted as the obstruction to progress. In this scenario, as the colonizer, the hegemonic settler, conquered and appropriated the Peoples in the New World, the Indigenous were progressively disenfranchised. This resulted in the creation of the "other" and a commensurate system that was upheld throughout the centuries. Thus, "the Indian Problem must be understood as part of a stage and intellectual movement that tried to explain the life and marginalization of the Indigenous Peoples. Yet these very explanations were oppressive principles because they invisibilized and racialized us, eventually leading to our position as inferior juveniles, unable to resist the oppression."[15]

In fact, the 1990s in Latin America was the decade that marked the most important Indigenous uprisings of the twentieth century. Indigenous Peoples have organized and continue to rise up in opposition to this "ignominious treatment."[16] Pueblos have realized that it is time to take over and transform the state, with their participation at the highest levels. The ongoing backlash and desire to contain Indigenous access to power is part of a State and elitist discourse to negate any opposition. In response, resistance movements in the Americas have been galvanized, bringing people from all walks of life to protest events such as DAPL, Bears Ears, football games, genocide, sexual violence, and racial slurs.

Lucia Xiloj takes the entire issue of "the Indian Problem" and recasts it in the current moment as a necessary reversal of the handling and labeling of the Indigenous as objects.

> We have moved beyond talking about the "Indigenous Problem" to talking more about the rights of the Indigenous peoples, because "Indigenous Problem" is one of the many terms which does not come from the Indigenous communities themselves. Right now, at least in Guatemala, there is an important understanding that the Indigenous people have stopped being a mere object of study. That is why I am very interested in what you were saying at the beginning about autoethnography, because I have always been critical of those that came to study the Indigenous population as if we were objects. Whereas now we are the ones identifying and discussing the situations that we believe threaten our rights, the fabric of our communities, and the conditions of the people. That is why it is more about the vindication of rights than the "Indigenous Problem."[17]

The contemporary "Indian Problem" might well be very different from the historical "problem," as the Indigenous assume positions of power—protagonists and agents of their own destiny.

Notes

1 Betasamosake Simpson, Indigenous Resistance.
2 Loring, in discussion with the author, 2018.
3 Tulley-Cordova, in discussion with the author, October 18, 2017.
4 de la Torre Amaguaña, in discussion with the author, December 5, 2016.
5 Tubin, in discussion with the author, September 29, 2017.
6 Batzibal, in discussion with the author, September 25, 2017.

7 Interview with activist, discussion with author in confidentiality, name withheld by mutual agreement, December 11, 2017.
8 Interview with activist, discussion with author in confidentiality, name withheld by mutual agreement, 2017.
9 Presley, "Embodied Liminality and Gendered State Violence," 91–109.
10 Barson, "Artivism and Decolonization."
11 Cumes, in discussion with the author, September 24, 2017.
12 Benito, in discussion with the author, September 29, 2017.
13 Hernández, in discussion with the author, September 28, 2017.
14 Curruchich, in discussion with the author, September 28, 2017.
15 Velasquez Nimatuj, "Indigenous Women and Activism."
16 Hernández, in discussion with the author, September 28, 2017.
17 Xiloj, in discussion with the author, September 24, 2017.

5 Social Sciences

The role of Western social sciences in relation to Indigenous People was an integral part of these interviews as the women addressed social scientific practice within their own domain of knowledge and from their locus of enunciation in the last few years.

The May 2013 guilty verdict (vacated that same month) in the genocide trial of ex-President Rios Montt in Guatemala, and the outcome of the 2016 Presidential election in the United States and its aftermath, raised questions about the failure of social science. Both events exposed paradoxical behavior and excused racism and sexism in an apparent global resurgence of overt fascism. In these cases, right-wing populist politics dominated. The battle against sexual rights found an ally in US politics, underwritten by ultra-conservative leanings. Gender studies might have, and may still, shed light on how a man of Trump's economic stature could treat women in a demeaning, denigrating manner and still garner support from women in a democratic, informed electorate. Likewise, critical race theory might explain how oppressed people support authoritarian regimes, even in the case of mass murder targeted at their group. In this context, the social sciences take on significance in the exposure of previously-silenced voices and the mandate to recognize marginalized populations and the commensurate rights of diverse peoples on a global scale. But an erosion of credible, legitimate researched knowledge in the social sciences also seems to be in the offing.

The contradictions surrounding these two events elicited a profound revalorization, one that had been in the making for many of these women, regarding the colonization and cooption of social scientific methodology. Linda T. Smith, in *Decolonizing Research Methodologies*, and other theorists, have probed this same topic.[1] The ideas presented here survey the social sciences as a way to assess inroads toward comprehending their biases and democratizing their *modus operandi.*

The methodology of disciplines in the social sciences is aligned with the examination of individual and collective identity—we are social, political, ethnic, racial, and gendered subjects. The questioning of the disciplines by these women germinated in a kind of grounded research, spawning the meta-analysis presented here, as the interviewees scrutinized their own fields and highlighted problems and solutions. The women delved into the conceptual and methodological manipulation of Western science and the problematic repercussions of bias in social science methods.

Intrigued by the issues raised in the 2016 election and by the words of these women, I reflected upon my own training. I am a Northern-centered Latina literary scholar, whose learning spans both humanities and social sciences, epistemologies of the North and South, and is grounded in multidisciplinarity as a primary modality. Looking into the role of social sciences in contemporary rationality was not something that arose naturally in my intellectual inquiries. My primary field of humanities must continuously defend a *raison d'etre* and justification for pragmatic, fiscal, and curricular viability. Conversely, and naively interrogated on my part, social sciences from afar had appeared more stable and poised to remain aloof from threats of these material financial and practical indictments, by nature of a presumed scientific, objective, and quantitative grounding.

From its inception, sociology, generated from the positivist framework, was an academic discipline concerned with empirical practice and what could be observed. Theories on social life were derived from fixed and circumscribed variables of testable, validated fact. Irrefutable gauges for objectively surveying the truth about the way society functions could, it was believed, be crafted. Yet early naysayers, like Arthur Stinchcombe (1933–2018), anticipated the possible shortcomings of the discipline, especially where humans were transformed into *objects* of sociological study.[2] Some anthropologists also, questioning the procedure and premise of anthropological studies, quantifiability of culture, and impossibility of objective field or theoretical work, were careful to disavow a biased rationalization and application of an objective science that might justify hierarchies between ethnic and racial groups.

Others have tried to determine potential contributions to an intellectual understanding of the human condition as well as the devastating repercussions portended for certain groups leveled as objects by Western social science. Early on, Peruvian social critic Jose González de Prada (1844–1918) in his essay, "Our Indians," admonished that the objective of ethnology might end up as a means in which: "…one grants the division of humanity into superior and inferior races and recognizes the superiority of the whites and their consequent right to govern the planet, nothing is more natural than the suppression of the Black in Africa, the Redskin in the United States, the Tagalog in the Philippines, or the Indian in Peru."[3]

With the rise of interdisciplinarity and interculturality, the exchange of broad-ranging perspectives emanating from discrete fields has led to the assessment of the contributions and deficits of the social sciences. Profound, complex global and local problems need viable solutions. Integrating non-Western knowledge and decolonizing existing subjective methods of studying individual and collective identity within the social sciences may be the only way to promote a sustainable and more equitable representation and analysis of research. Diverse knowledge systems, epistemologies, and approaches must be present throughout conversation, decision-making, and action. Dr. Pam Palmater, LASA-ERIP (Latin American Studies Association-Ethnicity, Race and Indigenous Peoples) Gonzaga 2019 keynote speaker, entreated: "Indigenous women and individuals of color must have an authoritative say and role in all kinds of discussions beyond Native women's role in the domestic domain."[4] Furthermore, social science must understand the human element implicit in the scientific sphere and democratize its processes. Interviewees Liliana Hernández, De la Torre Amaguaña, Aura Cumes, Victoria Tubin, and others speak of humanizing law, humanizing pedagogy with an infusion of *interculturalidad*, and decolonizing their professions which are bound by Western social scientific methodologies.

To this same point, Donna Loring recalled her military service as an 18-year-old in Vietnam as communications specialist logging region casualties. She began to extrapolate these figures from her situation as a Native woman in the United States: "The military taught us to dehumanize people in order to consider them animals to kill more easily. It has been my life's objective since that realization to humanize my people. I have tried many ways to do that."[5]

Expert witnesses and lawyers for survivors of sexual violence and ethnic cleansing campaigns reinforce the notion that the social sciences have to help humanize law and the justice system. The role of these systems is not only to provide justice to communities or people; it is, above all, to humanize them, albeit years later. Lucia Xiloj claims there is no other way to prove a survivors' truth, and reaffirm these events before the judicial tribunal. It is a methodology of collaboration between survivors of genocide and committed researchers that decolonizes the institutions and systems of justice and restitution, and the methodology of their practices.[6] The methodology, struggles and obstacles of Indigenous Peoples in Guatemala in these cases of "demanding justice and confronting members of the state's security apparatus" are laid bare in the recent work in the judicial system that is engaged in such humanization and civil rights advocacy.[7]

Luz Maria de la Torre Amaguaña, scholar of Quechua and Andean epistemologies at UCLA, applies these ideas to education.

> This new form of liberation, an emancipating pedagogy, impacts them [the students] profoundly. The students begin to see their real problems through this analysis. In this class, they combine methods of analysis with this experience of the Indigenous from the Andean area. They learn vast amounts, and immediately put it into action.
>
> It also puts their lives in perspective. They question themselves, racism, social stratification, the space in which they are developing. It is part of the process to humanize Pedagogy. We work from that premise. If not, they only collect theories, which need to be put into practice. I problematize this, and try to put this all into crisis for them.
>
> They have to explore how to solve a problem, not only from a theoretical point of view, rather practical, from questioning the ink on their papers, the water they drink, from the cup of coffee, to where it came from? It asks them to question their own actions in life and what solutions they can offer in the real world. We need to shift from complaint to proposing solutions. The Indigenous are doing precisely that in order to effectuate change and transformation.[8]

In education, diminishing resources, coupled with the evaluation of the role, impact, and methodologies of one discipline or cohort of relational subjects and approaches over another, has become pervasive and rancorous. No discipline is immune from scrutiny. Value and function in the West are driven by quantitative measures and profits as well as power politics. Academic disciplines calculate metrics and quantifiable values for intangibles such as language, culture, social investments, and more. Yet epistemologies of the Good Life (*Buen Vivir, Minobimaatisiiwin, Sumak Kawsay*) eschew fiduciary quantification. Rather, these alternative knowledge systems adamantly propose the reorganization and realignment of human integrity, social-justice, equality, and integrative conceptualizations of well-being as primary stakeholders required at the table of adjudication of social sciences.

The current imperative to examine questions addressed by social science from distinct interwoven perspectives in order to solve complicated, large-scale problems has elicited the adoption of a more holistic approach, focused on the interaction of expertise across two or more disciplines and epistemologies, a decolonization of methodology. This necessitates opening exchange and interconnection through integrative approaches. It entails representation of diversity and inclusivity that rejects vertical, colonial hierarchical privileging in favor of horizontality. Indigenous epistemologies have consistently advanced the concepts of *interculturalidad*, reciprocity, and complementarity as innate protocols. Given that problems are transdisciplinary, like solutions must follow suit. With global challenges facing the environment, biodiversity, social systems, humanistic interaction and communication, the role and inputs of various intellectual traditions and knowledge systems, as well as qualitative and quantitative reasoning must be taken into account.

A participant of the United Nations Permanent Forum on Indigenous Issues (UNPFII or PFII), comments on racism against Indigenous peoples, and offers an analysis of rationale for cross-sectionality of Indigenous identity, gender, and ethnicity.

> Knowledge is very important for our struggles—for anthropology, sociology, social work. The question is how to realize this interdisciplinarity so as to advance concrete proposals. If we changed from not only approaching problems from a discrete discipline, rather adopting an integrated perspective, with the social sciences, legal studies, administration, economics, psychology, with all of these amalgamated, we could advance satisfactorily. However, that is precisely the opposite of what happens since we must specialize in particular disciplines, which impedes our ability to interrelate and correlate our knowledge.
>
> Ultimately, we clash. This is the current problem, even though it is not specific to only the social sciences. With credibility and accountability disputed in the public domain since 2016, it is vital to focus attention on how and where narratives of historical import are legitimized. Colonized methodologies must be scrutinized for results that might be inadequate, ineffectual, specious, or which have been coopted or compromised to solely represent hegemonic interests.
>
> Although much discriminatory behavior and opaque racist societal structures seem normalized today, it is through analysis of those oppressive inequitably-

> distributed advantages and their ramifications, that a more accurate functionality of social sciences is brought to light.[9]

This backdrop set the tone and themes for the inquiry about possible failures of the social scientific community to predict and explain correctly the current epoch. Necessarily, the question of the role of the social sciences emerged. Several women drew upon their perception of the cooptation of social science, such that this presumed-objective science has served primarily to advance a knowledge base for rightwing political interests. Having been trained in academic institutions in doctoral studies of social science, Indigenous researchers are acutely aware of their precarious position of intersectionality vis-a-vis ethnicity, gender, socio-economics, and geopolitical fracturing. Moreover, the tools of the doctoral field in which they practice were the same used, in some cases, to oppress the Indigenous people. The colonial cooptation of social science is a common theme espoused. Many point out the direct threats undermining affirmative action and diversity initiatives, or the ongoing efforts to essentialize ethnic inferiority and bolster racism through scientific formulations. The dangerous resurgence of white supremacy movements and neofascism empowered an augmented blatant bigotry and discrimination within many discourses, including those of the social sciences. Not unlike the yellow journalism of the late nineteenth century, fear-based and propagandistic news sources, as much as a political distortion of data, challenge the discernment of truth from fiction and vitriol.

Theorists were questioning these pernicious approaches in the early twenty-first century. Studies such as *White Logic, White Methods*; *Thicker Than Blood: How Racial Statistics Lie*; *Race Relations: A Critique*, or *Decolonizing European Sociology: Transdiciplinary Approaches*, and others presented compelling arguments for a revamping of the social sciences.[10] More contemporary researchers have actively sought to expose and dismantle the narrow research parameters of Western-based study. *Decolonizing Ethnography: Undocumented Immigrants and New Directions in Social Science*,[11] for instance, offers a methodological and theoretical reassessment of social science, examining how it can function as a vehicle for activism and as a tool for marginalized people.

These scholarly denunciations peel back the racial lenses of the social sciences and the implicit biases, conscious and/or not, that social scientists have subscribed to from European methodologies which perpetuate and scaffold the "race effect" on knowledge production, data analysis, and policy determinations.

The conversations here explored the tension inherent between Indigenous identity, and the training and implementation of social scientists grounded in hegemonic structural and methodological bias. Indigenous attorneys, sociologists, anthropologists, journalists, educators, advisors to international governing agencies, performers, media broadcasters, youth organizers, and legislators discuss the need to decolonize methods and findings that support only the propagation of dominant culture, male patriarchal power, and elites while further subjugating marginalized ethnic, racial, and socioeconomic groups throughout the Americas. For them, the social sciences remain at the service of interests and structures that have been repressive and employed as justification for genocide, gender subjugation, stratification, and ethnic/racial division. The interviewees point out the various facets of their work that warrant decolonization, humanization, and rebalancing of the relationship between researcher and subject towards a more horizontal plane.

Aura Estela Cumes Simon, a social anthropologist, remarks:

> Generally speaking, the social sciences are the sciences most closely related to the struggles of the *campesinos*, to the social movements, and to the Indigenous people. They occupy various spaces depending on the context in which they are found. If we speak of Mexico, Mexican anthropology is to a large extent a traditional anthropology that sees the "subject" as barbarous, and perhaps with an element of paternalism or maternalism, and in that way the "subject" is studied.
>
> The time I spent in Mexico was immersed in an anthropology that was very much traditional and tends toward expropriation. In spite of our interaction with professors and our critiques waged within the classroom, many instructors would not cede to the possibility of viewing Indigenous subjects in the way that we claimed. They assumed the authority of giving their "subjects" the place that they as social scientists wanted to give them. Thus, the anthropology that I had the opportunity to learn was very much colonial.
>
> There are exceptions—there are always groups of instructors that are doing everything in their power to decolonize the social sciences and establish a different relationship with their subjects. But doing everything they can does not mean serious contradictions are not present or that they are always listening to what the subject has to say.[12]

The central relationship that conventionally structures research models is between subject/object or informant/source in various fields. Juana Batzibal Tujal problematizes the social injustices of that traditional relationship and suggests an alternative, rectifying the power imbalance.

> Social science has taught us methodologies, techniques in which we see the individual as nothing more than an object. During the era of my studies, the concept

> of the "informant" was defined as exclusively a person who might be a subject of "legal scrutiny" or a "political subject." The relationship was of "I, the investigator," and that research subject was mere "informant."
>
> We have been trying to resolve that dilemma, in order to visualize research precisely where there is a different focus. It is a relationship of "you-you." As researcher, I know nothing more than the other person. I, the investigator, only know something different from those who convey it to me. The person gives me information they know, and in this manner, we complement one another, and that is the fundamental point.
>
> One of the basic principles of my work, and certainly fundamental to my culture, is complementarity. When we speak of complementarity, it is not necessarily only between men and women. It is the complementarity between humanity and nature, which in our research is "subject: investigator." Both of us convert to status of political subjects, if we really want to impose a positive application onto all scientific knowledge.
>
> To this extent, the word decolonize is key—how are we going to apply science from any perspective instead of speaking of knowledge from the imperious egocentrism predominant now, rather can we adopt a collective standpoint?[13]

These women underscore the processes of revitalization, reorientation, revalorization, resignification, and resemantization of Indigenous identity in the decolonization of social science methodology. The transcendence of disciplinary boundaries and methodological frameworks, specifically a bridging of the divide between praxis and theory and hierarchies of who can theorize, so as to provide space for self-representation of all populations, is expressed as a core value. In the 1980s, Chicana Gloria Anzaldúa encouraged non-white theorists to "de-academize theory and to connect the community to the academy" and, in turn, bear in mind multiple ways of theorizing as valid[14]. Drawing on this notion, literary scholar Elizabeth A. Archuleta (Yaqui/Chicana) in "'I Give You Back': Indigenous Women Writing to Survive," stresses that Indigenous women theorize in their own and different ways, and through their own experiences. Academic methodology, epistemology, and cross-disciplinary training, but not solely, provide a way of speaking to each other, the Indigenous community, and to other communities. Contrasting a European patriarchal model, Indigenous women "have crafted oppositional knowledge designed to resist oppression."

They rely on more than "Western tools, worldviews, or epistemologies as methods of interpretation. Indigenous women reject paradigms that ask us to disassociate ourselves from our lived experiences before we can claim to have the skills and knowledge to theorize. We believe theory comes not from abstract written ideas but from the collective knowledge of Indigenous women whose lives have not informed feminist theories, methods, or policy concerns and whose lived experiences mainstream feminists will continue to ignore unless Indigenous women question and deconstruct existing methodologies."[15]

The evaluation of the utility and function of social science is generated from a non-privileged perspective, honing the implementation and integration of its tools in the realm of social justice, action, and change work. The assessment raises consciousness on gaps in knowledge, theory, and praxis, which impact both hegemonic and suppressed groups. As de la Torre Amaguaña states, "We must delegitimize these differences based on colonial oppression once and for all, and dismantle difference based on race, color, social status that are colonial vestiges of oppression."[16] Beyond theorization, change work must effectuate tangible results.

A distinct approach is to bring Ancestral Knowledge Systems from the local context into play on the broader geo-environmental theatre. Diné geologist Crystal Tulley-Cordova conducts water research on her tribal reservation. She contextualizes her findings and their applications. Her point of departure is the local, micro-setting from which she necessarily extrapolates onto the macro level in order to understand the global impact of the ecological issues surrounding water. Opposed to European theorization that is imposed on the "other," she turns the tables on the paradigms.

> The Navajo Nation is really reliant upon water. All human beings are reliant upon water for sustainability. I see my research as an opportunity to investigate a semi-arid to arid area, but an area that is very similar to other areas throughout the world. Water is an important resource for everyone: people, animals and plants. There's great impact that my research could have, not only for the Navajo community, but for the rest of the world.[17]

Bolivian, part-Aymara S. Rivera Cuscicanqui has argued in her writing that intellectual work involves certain risk, physical and intellectual, to the extent that social scientific research inherently must question the very base structures of power and reveal the integral way in which this investigation lays bare the inner workings of discrimination against women and Indigenous People. In other words, the need for meta-analysis of social sciences is crucial for social transformation to occur, yet it is dangerous, far beyond only existing in the logocentric sphere. Cuscicanqui, along with Esther Diaz, proposes the imposition of an ethical platform onto social scientific research.[18] The implication of such a theoretical conceptualization is far-reaching, just as active protests are events of contention and resistance.

The premise of European social sciences lies in unearthing the attributes and dynamics of social relations, taken only to involve humans, whereas positionality and definitions of social subjectivity are more robust in other worldviews. Within Indigenous epistemologies, subjectivity transcends humans to include animals and all of nature. A more inclusive knowledge-base for social science must engage in the examination and enrichment of social relations amongst humans but include equally the natural world. Unlike the European view of human domination, exploitation, consumption, and subjugation, the Indigenous conception of social interaction and subjectivity fosters a distinct holistic, reciprocal relationship between human, animal, and natural entities.

To make social science what Velásquez Nimatuj calls "a subversive space" real,[19] a fusion of activism and academics, in which both contribute important knowledge for change, is essential. Moreover, the space will find cohesion between theory and praxis, as public change makers and academics collaborate in tandem. Some Indigenous social scientists argue that it is also their role to be activists, while others focus solely on disseminating information. Various interviewees endorse the radicalization and politicization of the social sciences. In part, this is because the social sciences offer tools in critical race and gender theory to combat encroaching patriarchal discrimination. Social sciences are understood as an intellectual apparatus that helps to unveil and dismantle the effects and logic of the "Intimate Enemy"—the insidious internalization and colonization of the mind.[20] Not only deleterious to the colonized when imposed psychologically by the colonizer, the oppressed Indigenous/women/periphery might replicate the oppression waged against them onto their own or may even support a regime that perpetrates genocide or violence against them. Social sciences may help us find an effective means for understanding this. Yet, meta-analysis of these tools, criteria, and rationale suggests the subjective biases of research design and appropriation remain exclusively oriented to, and executed by, elitist goals. Activist anthropology or other engaged, committed academic research could be a channel or conduit to contest the usurpation of methodology that preserves the status quo, and, contrariwise, might serve to illuminate oppression. Throughout all of these interviews, the women emphasize the importance of a more egalitarian and decolonized approach in which social scientists and Indigenous communities interact in a mutual exchange of ideas and then use the mutually-gleaned knowledge to create proposals for the future.

A Maya K'iche' lawyer frames her understanding of the role of social sciences this way:

> Social sciences definitely have an important role to play. Apart from legal applications, there is the issue of monitoring sociological matters, of identifying how these dynamics take place. For example, when discussing the relationship between the United States and Guatemala, the topic of immigration is important, of how that phenomenon takes place. It is significant on many levels because it changes the situation of Indigenous communities. Oftentimes, in spite of what they gain in the United States in the form of economic advances, no change occurs in people's living conditions, because they receive no help from consultants on how to invest their economic resources, or on what priorities they should focus on.[21]

The social sciences can help identify oppressive structural barriers and dismantle them. For many of the interviewees the goal of the social scientific inquiry should be with an eye to social justice and the betterment of society.

> As science, as disciplines, they should always be at the service of society. The issue is not about the science itself as much as the people who devise and administer the sciences. In many cases, the social scientists utilize their knowledge against the people in our pueblos. We have experienced this situation clearly in Guatemala, because even some of our Maya brothers and sisters with academic backgrounds have been coopted in that way. In terms of economics, it has a similar impact on the Indigenous peoples. In our country, knowledge is not valued, and those who attempt to educate themselves are not recognized for the effort they put into their education. Thus, because their employment does not carry much economic value, the companies abuse and exploit workers. The companies have more resources and know the importance of pocketing people from the community in order to secure more profit. Therefore, the first thing they do is coopt many. They offer them key positions, in theory, because in reality they are not given decision-making power. However, by means of providing them a salary in essence that is much better than they would normally have with our organizations, necessity obligates our brothers to cross over to the other side. Unfortunately, then they put their knowledge to use for the corporation, rather than for our organizations. We have witnessed this on various fronts.
>
> Therefore, in their purest form, the social sciences are good. Any science is valuable to the extent that it is applied reasonably. Yet we realize the economic reality, as in the case of University of San Carlos, which is an institution that had historically been in solidarity with the Indigenous people, yet 16 years ago they were coopted and disappeared from our struggle. This is to say, it is not so much

that the social sciences are dysfunctional, rather the issue concerns how the social sciences are manipulated and used as tools of oppression by individuals. [22]

Journalist Victoria Tubin adds:

It is remarkable to say this, but it appears that in this day and age of globalization, the social sciences do not carry the same value or meaning as before, and might even be eroding or eliminated. However, at the same time, this situation may serve as a strategy in some perverse way because the social sciences are contributing theoretically and epistemologically.

Certain tools permit us to comprehend these current and historical contexts, and the structural barriers existing today in our society, not only in Guatemala or the United States, rather worldwide. Obviously, the social sciences must pass through a type of codification, because up until now they have focused on eurocentrism and Occidentalism, instead of being a social science based on the inclusive contributions and knowledge of those excluded from the production of scientific knowledge, silenced, or viewed as subalterns. Therefore, the challenge for the social sciences is also how to construct a social science that is not only western, rather more expansive, with the caveat of democratizing knowledge.

How do we understand knowledge and not-knowledge? There is absolutely nothing which can be characterized as not knowledge, even though the Eurocentric academics teach us that precise fallacy.[23]

Antonia Benito, radio journalist for Radio Qawinaqel, which broadcasts in the community's native language, spoke to the decolonizing efforts taking place in her milieu. She suggests that working within the community in native Mayan language, and in the surrounding areas, is a way to reinforce this process. Through radio broadcasts and coverage of local projects, in the local to the national realms, the broadcasts corroborate the advances. "The media is fundamental to being able to create criteria, to be able to facilitate tools or panoramas that show what is happening."[24] For her, media should make people's lives easier. However, broadcasters must evaluate the evidence that the media uses to transmit information, because of the potential to manipulate information.[25] In her community work she is a strong advocate for the social media platforms that offer new methods of disseminating, and better control over content dissemination.

Regarding challenges facing her Nation, a former staff member of an Indigenous environmental justice organization and DAPL organizer/protester indirectly addresses the chasms in social science knowledge production.

> Institutional racism comes in varying forms ... we lack the necessary education to succeed within this racism. We often lack the resources, and the champions in our community to make or leverage any resources that do come in, a viable resource for our communities.
>
> We have severely limited access to so many resources supposedly made available to us though we are underserved communities. Institutional racism is one of those issues we face. Severe mental health disorders, which no one looks into, because we are being undersold to begin with. On top of the racism, people often look at our communities and assume we are lazy. However, we are communities that have been systematically traumatized via verbal abuse, sexual assault, emotional abuse we face from our educators, law enforcement, health care professionals who have sterilized our women.
>
> Other exploitation in the form of church communities that come into our homelands and brainwash our children and even sexually assault them. One of the biggest threats is outsiders, not the Native people, but the non-native, mostly white communities that come in with their god complexes, thinking that they are going to be able to save us or help us in some capacity, but, ultimately, they only end up doing more damage than good. They have a need to service their own guilt.
>
> I would hope white guilt would stay out of our communities, because all it does is takes us further away from the end goal of recovering from what their ancestors did to us. It takes three generations to flush trauma out of your blood memory and we can't even get one generation away from our most recent traumas!
>
> From there stems the reality: fossil fuels infrastructure is built and the man-camps accompany them. Then comes the influx of drugs that enter into the community to service the man camps. Think about how the pipelines impact our communities and ground water supplies, leading to higher carcinogens and rates of cancer. When those go up, more children are born with cancer or birth defects. The list goes on. It's not a matter of what the largest challenges are, rather what *isn't* impacting our communities.[26]

Integration of Indigenous epistemologies into conventional social science paradigms and procedure could potentially lend these sciences a distinct countenance. De la Torre Amaguaña describes *Yanantin* as a non-Western methodology, which could amplify the solutions.

> Yanantin is another useful concept. It's a good way for groups to find alliances. It is an agricultural practice, in reality. We, the Indigenous, have nourished much of our experience from being farmers, the space and practice where we have to do our own daily work and planting. We have been able to reinterpret and apply the elements of tending to the earth in other directions. Yanantin in agriculture

means that when planting corn, maize grows, and we must pack soil in to support that plant, so that the wind doesn't blow it over. The land that supports the sprouts from each side is called Yanantin, a complementary dualism. It's a metaphor that helps you understand all the behaviors of life. When a man and woman [or other couples] come together, [he] is a Yanan, because they both support each other in order to sustain the family and to support their own interests.

This is Yanantin. When we strive to unite these two groups, Western society and the so-called Indigenous, it will resemble and function like Yanantin. We are finding that way through a common goal that is held by two forces. Yanantin does not necessarily have to be entities with the same thought, rather they may be different. It is more or less what in the West is called the dialectic, understood as an eternal struggle of opposites. You will never be able to join or consolidate them in union. Impossible. There is no way to reconcile.

However, Yanantin from the Andean conception are complete opposites, though those opposites are intimately united. The word Yanantin comes from Yanapana which means to help. The suffix "intin" means an inseparable union: opposites, but united. That is the [man and the woman], because the [man] and the [woman] are two completely different entities in all areas, and yet by love they unite. For love they are together, in spite of all differentiation. That's Yanantin.

As for the Europeans, they must start listening. Even so, they have to start to hear other voices. Our voice must be heard. Listen to the South, listen to the Indigenous voice, listen to the voices of Indigenous women. That is, without meaning "yours is not worth listening to," because that is not our intention.

Yanantin works. The two forms begin to coexist. Patricio Guerrero Arias, an Ecuadorian sociologist, developed this idea of the union of these two forces, of heart and reasoning. Academics are full of the reasoning function. Academe is pure reasoning, leading it to forget the heart, passion, and emotion. Meanwhile, our culture has a lot of emotion and heart. These two forces must merge, it is important. Passion and reason, combined with heart and affection cannot be undone either.

These things together can make a rational, as well as emotional, human being. For example, any knowledge, thought, or reasoning together with other theories, for instance high ethics and morals, emotion, and gratitude would be ideal. The contributing factor is the Yanantin. Our collaboration group has tried to convert these ideas into pedagogy, where the heart and temporal reasoning come together.[27]

Some of the interviewees study in the social sciences so as to be familiar with the oppressor. Liliana Hernández, a lawyer working on Guatemalan Civil War abuses, chose to get close to the systems she identified as powerful yet inaccessible to the Indigenous.

> With respect to the discipline or science of law, we must remember that it is constructed in a way that ensures the reproduction of the state. It has been very difficult for me to engage with the educational blueprint of the university, in which they force us to replicate and be custodians and guardians of this racist and oppressive state, and not to question these laws and this nation.
>
> I have had many disagreements with other lawyers since graduating, because I consider myself a rebellious lawyer—I question the laws, I do not replicate them. The laws should be formed by the people, by their necessities. If not, the laws will form the people. That is why I believe that with respect to laws and rights, there are enormous challenges in Guatemala and in other countries that have imposed these models, where there are native peoples with justice systems that have distinct logics in which our communities resolve problems through agreements and mediation, and not through punishment or punitive measures.
>
> This model which has legal [standing] is entirely different from the vision of the native peoples and of women. If we talk about how the laws do or do not protect Indigenous women from my experience in the Defensoría de la Mujer Indígena in the department of Totonicapán, the measures of protection for women that are written in law do not really apply, because they have no access to police, to phone service, or to a justice system. For that reason, women and their families turn to the Indigenous authorities.
>
> They are opposite realities, distinct logics. Speaking of the social sciences, the current challenge is to deeply understand those forms of solving problems and to leave them be, to let the people have their own forms of organization and their own view of life. What has happened is that there has been an imposition on every level, not only from the perspective of languages and a political system, but also an entire way of thinking. I chose to be trained as a lawyer precisely because I had to know how the nation that oppresses us works, so I could transform it.[28]

These interviews draw attention to the dangers of expropriation/ appropriation that social scientists face when they view Indigenous people as subjects of study and the social scientist as an artificial wielder of power. The women argue for social scientists to validate the Indigenous as equals who are fighting, along with social scientists, for a better life, potentially adhering to the model of participatory action research. They encourage a decolonization of concepts and methods.

Notes

1 Smith, *Decolonizing Research Methodologies.* See also Kovach, *Indigenous Methodologies*; Quijano, "Coloniality of Power;" Pérez Huber, "Challenging Racist Nativist Framing;" Pérez Huber, "Disrupting Apartheid of Knowledge;" Tuck, "Rational Validity and the 'Where' of Inquiry;" Alonso Bejarano, *Decolonizing Ethnography.*
2 Stinchcombe, "The Origins of Sociology as a Discipline."
3 Gonzalez Prada, "Our Indians."
4 Palmater, ["Keynote Speech"].
5 Loring, in discussion with the author, 2018.
6 https://soundcloud.com/bea-gallardo-shaul/sets/dra-irma-alicia-vel-quez
7 Clacso, "La lucha de las mujeres por la igualdad en América Latina y el Caribe."
8 de la Torre Amaguaña, in discussion with the author, December 5, 2016.
9 Batzibal Tujal, in discussion with the author, September 25, 2017.
10 Tukufu, White Logic, White Methods; Tukufu, Thicker Than Blood; Steinberg, Race Relations; Gutiérrez Rodríguez, Decolonizing European Sociology.
11 Alonso Bejarano, Decolonizing Ethnography.
12 Cumes, in discussion with the author, September 23, 2017.
13 Batzibal Tujal, in discussion with the author, 2017.
14 Anzaldua, Making Face, Making Soul/HaciendoCaras, xxv.
15 Archuleta, "'I Give You Back,'" 95–114, 89.
16 de la Torre Amaguaña, in discussion with the author, December 5, 2017.
17 Tulley-Cordova, in discussion with the author, October 18, 2017.
18 Díaz, "Algunas Consideraciones Para Una Ética Aplicada a La Investigación Científica."
19 Velasquez, https://www.colectivasos.com/integrantes/irma-velasquez/
20 Nandy, *The Intimate Enemy.*
21 Xiloj, in discussion with author, September 24, 2017.
22 Interview with attorney, discussion with author in confidentiality, name withheld by mutual agreement, 2017.
23 Tubin, in discussion with the author, September 29, 2017.
24 Benito, in discussion with the author, September 29, 2017.
25 Prensa, Entrevista.
26 Interview, discussion with author in confidentiality, name withheld by mutual agreement, November15, 2017.
27 de la Torre Amaguaña, in discussion with the author, 2017.
28 Hernández, in discussion with the author, September 28, 2017.

6 Being an Indigenous Woman

The women interviewed in this book reflect on the honor and respect with which they hold their culture, their pride in Indigenous legacy, and the implications for their identity in the twenty-first century.

Aura Cumes refers to possibilities.

> I do not speak from the perspective of an identity, but from a condition. Yesterday I was rereading the words of Ginés de Sepúlveda when he and Bartolomé de las Casas were debating whether or not the Indians had souls. Sepúlveda said that "the Indians are slaves by nature, as the animal is to man, as the wife is to the husband, as the son is to the father," etc. What he was trying to understand was a completely hierarchical world, which for him is the nature of the legitimate order of things. We are living in a world perfectly structured in that way, where hierarchies make a lot of sense. But in that hierarchical chain, we Indigenous women are placed on the lowest rung. For a long time, I have been questioning feminism and gender theory, because every time it tries to study violence against women, it goes to the domestic arena. In the home, this theory sees the Indigenous men as the culprits, which obfuscates State violence and institutional violence against men, the violence transpiring in the public domain and streets where Indigenous men are not the victimizers. Now, if we keep the place of Indigenous women in mind (and here I refer to the comadronas and the tejedoras, and to the women

> who were violently raped during the war), and we observe how power is structured around women, we realize that any human being who is ranked higher on the power structure can dispossess her in any way. A ladino man can dispossess her; a ladina woman or a foreigner can dispossess an Indigenous person, and Indigenous men and women in "better" economic conditions can do the same. Indigenous women are the lowest in this hierarchy. They have the possibility of being displaced in so many ways. How can we visibilize domination from that place? It is important to construct it, and it is exactly what we are doing with the tejedoras and comadronas. It is not the same to observe the domination from a place of privilege, like a ladino man, a ladina woman, or a foreigner who observes the oppression in this country.
>
> Therefore, our place in society is one of multiple dispossessions, but these multiple dispossessions give us the possibility, if we do it consciously, to analyze the power in myriad ways, and therefore we have the possibility of laying out a way of understanding domination, which is not one-dimensional. Instead, it gives us the chance to discover the various aspects. However, we are not the ones who produce epistemologies, science, or politics, and for that reason, every person who wields that power, manages to add another dimension of what they see from their perspective. If we, Indigenous women were able to speak, to render the shape of the domination, and our vision of the possible solutions, we would make an important contribution from the place of multiple displacements in which we have been located. We could also have a place in which we would be able to contribute to the understanding and to the solution of an issue that in this moment is only intelligible to a limited extent. We have the historical possibility of a distinct struggle. In terms of identity, I do not know. I am not going to start folklorizing or romanticizing. I leave it that we face many struggles in which we are involved.[1]

Identity for Indigenous women emphasizes a respect for the past, a profound bond through matrilineal and cultural traditions still relevant today. Tradition is not only backward leaning; it straddles their future and their children's survival. Crystal Tulley-Cordova considers:

> Today being a Navajo Woman, or thinking about what it is to be a woman, especially a Navajo Woman, takes me back to the time when I had a Kinaaldá ceremony. A Kinaaldá ceremony is a puberty ceremony, a coming-of-age ceremony. I think about all those songs that were sung by the Medicine Man on my behalf the last night of the ceremony. Those songs were of Changing Woman ('Asdzą́ą́ Nádleehé). I remember how hard I had to work for those 3 days of my life, grinding over 100 pounds of corn by stone grinder, and being with my paternal grandmother every day at our homestead to abide by the teachings that

> she grew up with, the teachings that she was passed down to me, about what it is to be a woman.
>
> To be a Navajo woman today to me is to be able to remember our sacred matrilineal role and accept the responsibility of bringing life into this world. Bringing life into this world is a sacred responsibility, and a sacred responsibility that is not to be taken lightly. That's why I'm really thankful for the partner that I have to raise my son. My son, not only is he Navajo, but he's Mexican. It's important to have him know both sides of where he comes from. To be a Navajo woman, I have that responsibility to be able to share all I know with him. I want him to know first he is Tódích'íi'nii. He is of the Bitter Water clan. He comes from a long line of prayers. I recognize that in myself, too. I am the corn pollen prayers of yesterday. The corn pollen prayers that were said in the early morning and the late nights by my ancestors that prayed for those who were to come after them, to make a difference in the world.[2]

The weight of ancestors' sacrifices guide the goals for many women. They engage with their communities and the heritage of other First Peoples. Education of the young in their lifeways and language is a large part of their duty. Cristina Marin examines the charge of this particular leadership role.

> I work in a secondary school, with a vulnerable population in terms of economics that consists of a high percentage of descendants of the First Peoples of the area. It is a school where the majority are not aware of, and do not recognize these rights of First Peoples, and deny them. Everything I alluded to before is part of that reality. As a Mapuche First People's woman, I carry a huge burden and responsibility to recover, preserve and promote our spirituality and philosophy. I have an opportunity in both schools where I teach to impart the philosophy of our people, educate them about our rights, and teach them our language Mapuzungun. That is what it means to me.[3]

Reciprocity, mutual support, and reverence for the contributions of all are core values. Identity is not individual, rather it is collective. The roles of women are multiple, and embraced with compassion and fierce loyalty as commanders of change and cultural resurgence. One interviewee proclaims her identity as an Indigenous woman as "Showing up more than anyone has before." She says:

> My grandmas laid a path, carried a lot of burdens, being closer to the process of removal and displacement from their homelands. Those traumas were very real for them, such as, the boarding and residential schools. They did as much as they could with what they were carrying. However, it is my job to do more than that,

> more than my mother survived, after their mothers. I have to show up today as a Native American woman, as a mother, an auntie, and a caretaker, and nurse, and protector. I have to show up and be the Mama Bear, the doctor, the provider, and sure there is food and people are clothed. I feel every Indigenous woman today is stretched beyond what we strove for before, when we just had what we needed to survive. It is our duty to make sure everyone makes it through alive, and also does well. It's also my duty to acknowledge that as an Indigenous woman I am uplifting my two-spirit, trans sisters, and making sure that they have space to hold of their own as well. There are many things we were doing because we are bringers of life, the original protectors and life givers, but now we are protectors and defenders more than ever. We can't just let it be our men anymore. It has come full circle, and we are required to fight together again, not just one or the other, rather all of us. Acknowledging the duality that exists between the feminine and masculine, and all that is between. Recognizing it is not just you or me, but all of us. Asking, "How can I uplift and support you?" That is the charge for Indigenous women today: to uplift and support others. [4]

Yet, the women are clear about the complicated nature of being Native, woman, and part of a long and complex heritage of colonization and a culture with its own series of issues ranging from patriarchy to a generational divide. They acknowledge the effects of poverty and alcoholism or drug-abuse on their lives as well. The ambiguity of identity as one strives for change is not glossed over. Callan Chythlook-Sifsof muses:

> What does it mean to be an Alaskan Yupik woman today for you? For me it seems like a lot of contradictions. I feel the strength of my people. Yesterday I stared at a picture of my great grandmother. In my village, there is a generation of women who are so beautiful, strong and rugged. I saw in an older generation of my grandpa's peers and friends growing up, a quiet strength and peace. I can't describe it. I feel that strength, assurance and knowledge as a woman. I feel the products of colonization; serious misogyny exists in the village nowadays. In commercial fishing, I have felt as a woman that I needed to fight to be recognized. I feel that difference between the older culture, the strength of that healthy womanhood, and the really dysfunctional part where there are huge rates of domestic violence. On a daily basis, verbal degradation of women from people I love and cherish. They are part of our Native culture, but do not practice the Native values. They practice the white values where it becomes an adulteration of the new Native value of what women are worth. Mostly I feel strength, then dysfunction, and sadness for many marginalized Native women. I look to my role models from when I was little. I feel gifted and blessed to be a Native woman.

> We are getting smarter in Alaska, even if there are many polarizations occurring there. I know we are lucky there because having spent time here in Utah on the reservation, I witnessed how accessible their land is to anyone from California to Washington DC. People can go there and buy land to live on. Whereas the Native people have what we call—ancient sun dance lands—Other people can buy property wherever they want. Certain lands have been taken away. The reservation began in the 1980s. It once was big. Slowly over time, when you look at the aerial maps, you can see the government and bureaucracy are literally taking away the lands. Land is the most important issue in Alaska, because we are thought of as having so much. We are seeing people move in rapidly, which is inevitable. We need to look carefully at our land, how we value it, and be sure we have the ability to determine what happens to it. It is all we have left. Once it's [land] gone, our culture will be eliminated. Thus, land in Alaska is the most important issue. I love being able to talk about these things, especially in Salt Lake, I feel privileged to have a venue to speak, tell their truth and reveal their perspective.[5]

For those coming from war-torn histories, the challenge of Indigenous womanhood is complex, and involves intense self-introspection as they examine individual, community, and the nations with whom they share geographic and political ties. The desire to rise from the abuse, racism, and genocide to revitalize their Indigenous roots is strong. Liliana Hernandez envisions empowerment:

> Being an Indigenous woman is a commitment to leaving a legacy for other Indigenous women, of having the courage to break patterns of discrimination and misogyny. It is not easy to do, even from where I am. It is a path of undoing discrimination that has had personal and familial costs. As an Indigenous woman, I am dedicated to continue contributing to the full exercise of women's rights, from what I do and from my testimony of struggle as a woman and as a professional. It is an enormous challenge, but I want to leave this legacy for my daughters, because I want my culture to stay alive. I love my culture. I am proud of my roots and I want them to continue in a dignified way. I do not want them to see us as a problem anymore, but as a marvelous culture, as our grandparents were, and as we are today. It is a responsibility and duty, but it is also a satisfaction of life both from my personal life and as a part of the Maya Quiché culture of which I form a part and of which I am very proud.[6]

Still others, frequently engaged on the international level, feel the onus of paving a way forward for harmony and sustainability as the paradigm for humans of all backgrounds and the natural world to which all are attached. Sara Curruchich finds encouragement in this endeavor.

> As an Indigenous woman? In some ways, it feels as if we are sacrificed. The role of an Indigenous woman is very important as well as the role of Indigenous people throughout the world. Our role is to be a part of the construction of the path of peace, of justice, of cosmic equilibrium, of human equilibrium, and of a connection with everything that surrounds us. We, as Indigenous women, although they deny us many things, must continue fighting for our grandmothers, for everything they fought for, for the women who are here now, and for the women who are coming. Why? We are that hope, we are the light, and we are that force.[7]

The sense of fulfillment in being an Indigenous woman—from an appreciation of their traditional adornment to the languages they speak provides a powerful example for a continuity of identity. Antonia Benito feels this as a guiding force.

> Being an Indigenous woman is an honor, because from the moment when we begin to communicate in our language, we know that all of this information that we are sharing completely changes its meaning when it's translated into Spanish. We know that we are so different from other cultures, but live with the same purpose—collective well-being—which is fundamental for our Indigenous communities as much as everyone else. The ability to communicate in different ways so that we can express ourselves is fundamental for us as Indigenous women, as is being proud of being able to wear our clothing without facing discrimination. Above all, we are becoming professionals more and more frequently, from within our own communities, better able to express and convey our identity.[8]

Identity is a social, political and cultural construct that shifts with each chapter of our lives. These women affirm their identity through their languages, their clothing, and their professions, all the while acknowledging an acceptance of who they are, not who they are not or what others want them to be. An anti-mascot change agent owns this autonomy:

> What does it mean to be a Diné woman in 2017? I don't know what is happening, if it's because of my age, or with a heightened sense of decolonization or this stage of life with children, or being a part of the advocacy movement, but I feel pride. I have a strong sense of being a woman, and understanding the power I have as a Diné woman. Asserting who I am as Indigenous and confronting patriarchal systems oppressing us. It is hurtful and frustrating at moments. Society does not teach us to be confident and self-aware. They tell us "you can't do this" or "it isn't that way" or "you cannot come into our space." However, I am comfortable being who I am, and being able to teach my kids to respect and honor who they are. Once long ago our community was comprised of strong women, who would not

> allow others to do these things to them. She was a provider for herself and community. She thought of herself as strong. I reclaim that spirit. Across the boards, as Native People, I recognize the barriers—need for decolonization, overcoming psychological trauma and everything we have internalized. If you bring 100 people into the room, ten will learn. Then those ten go out and teach another group. For me the question is how do we get the information out to our people so they can learn. At times, social work and behavioral health services do not allow for those conversations. I have over a decade of experience in social services. I create the safe space from which people can begin to heal.[9]

Though Europeans have placed the Indigenous in museums and history books as relics of the past, being an Indigenous woman is imbued with an acute insight of how vibrant and alive Indigenous cultures are. Their connection with the past and the very real present aspects of their indigeneity incites a purpose and comprehension of the ways they contribute to solving the issues of today. Victoria Tubin provides a stirring endorsement of the value of Indigenous women:

> I feel so proud to be a Maya Kaqchikel, especially when I know that the erroneous history they have taught us since primary school is not our history. When I have gone over my ancestor's history and was made aware of the accurate information about their lives, it is a beautiful history that stirs passion in me. I have strong, deep roots, and feel immense pride in this heritage. In contrast to a nation that denies us, which throughout time has violently treated us as women and Indigenous, considering us inferior, at times I have felt the arduousness of our course. Somedays it is worse, and yet, precisely in that despicable challenge, I find sources of courage and determination. In situations like this conversation, I am inspired with a light to continue onward and know this world must change for my sons and daughters, in order to live in a better world. As First Peoples, we do not seek to return to that pre-Columbian life as it was prior to colonization. However, we do request respect in a globalized world, and recognition. Moreover, Western society should acknowledge that we Indigenous have much to contribute, be it knowledge or other realms. If we were to create a different kind of society, a different world, we could live in equal harmony and prosperity.[10]

The women interviewed here give thoughtful, articulate expression to what being an Indigenous woman means. They have carried us on a path well-trodden by the ancestors before them, honoring the significance of the past and respecting, with heightened awareness, the implications of an ancient identity in the twenty-first century. It is a sacred path.

Essential issues differentiate, and yet unite, these women. Whether from continents far apart from each other or from the same country, each of them responded to the interview questions in their own way. There is a striking similarity of theme and the manner in which that message is expressed. At the same time, the nuances of local language and tribal affinity offer a palate of unique experiences and challenges. From the arid desert of the southwestern United States to the Amazon jungle to the still-isolated Alaskan mountains to a New England legislature, these women's voices act as amplifiers of national debates and idiosyncratic discourses within their fields.

The term "Indigenous woman" means something specific to each interviewee, yet there is harmony in their voices. From disavowing Indigenous identity for reasons of personal security to assimilating for professional success to militantly rejecting colonialism, the voices remain connected to their heritage—an intangible cultural marker that fortifies, leaving an enduring legacy for voices yet to come.

Davina Smith speaks of the path and of these voices:

> As a Native American woman or Diné woman, I grew up understanding who my people are. I grew up with my grandparents in a hogan which, to this day I would never, ever take back because it gave me an understanding that I have a path to follow, a path to lead, and that is of balanced harmony, walking in beauty. My grandmother once told me before she passed on, "when you become my age as an elder, you will need to have your own song to pass on. That song is of everything, of every stage of your life that you've overcome, whether it be hard trials or something like the birth of your kids, in education, activism. Make sure those are things that you have as you move on to be respected as an elder, as a grandmother." I carry her words.
>
> When I became a teenager, I wanted to lose my identity as a Native person. This resulted from the assimilation forced on us in the boarding school system. In that different world, which was a white man's world, I was afraid. I was ashamed of the color of my skin. I covered myself. I no longer spoke the language. I no longer went to the ceremonies. I no longer performed the dances.
>
> Then, when I became a woman and mom, I realized my need for my culture. I need my identity. I must know who I am to continue this process. Those are trials that I've come to understand. I wouldn't go back and change it in any way because it gives me strength.[11]

Notes

1 Aura Cumes, in discussion with the author, September 23, 2017.
2 Crystal Tulley-Cordova, in discussion with the author, October 18, 2017.
3 Cristina Marin, in discussion with the author, November 21, 2017.
4 DAPL activist, in discussion with the author, 2017.
5 Callan Chythlook-Sifsof, in discussion with the author, October 10, 2017.
6 Liliana Hernandez, in discussion with the author, September 28, 2017.
7 Sara Curruchich, in discussion with the author, September 28, 2017.
8 Antonia Benito, in discussion with the author, September 29, 2017.
9 Anti-mascot activist, in discussion with author, December 2017.
10 Victoria Tubin, in discussion with author, September 29, 2017.
11 Davina Smith, in discussion with author, November 9, 2017.

Bibliography

Adamson, Rebecca. 2016. "Enoughness: Indigenous Economics 101." October 3, 2016. https://www.youtube.com/watch?v=hWTA69MHGpA.

———. 2015. "Finding Innovation in Traditional Values." Ted Talks. TedMed, 10 September 2015. https://www.tedmed.com/talks/show?id=299415

———. 2005. "Land Rich Dirt Poor." In *The Color of Wealth: The Story Behind the US Racial Wealth Divide*, edited by Barbara Robles, et al. New York: The New Press.

———. Papers. Sophia Smith Collection of Women's History. Smith College, Northampton, Massachusetts.

———. "Profile of Rebecca Adamson." Women's Media Center.

———. 2017. "Rebecca Adamson: Global Activist for Indigenous People." MAKERS. Accessed December 2017. https://womensmediacenter.com/profile/rebecca-adamson

Alonso Bejarano, Carolyn, et al. 2019. *Decolonizing Ethnography: Undocumented Immigrants and New Directions in Social Science*. London: Duke University Press.

Amanda Blackhorse, Marcus Briggs-Cloud, Philip Gover, Jillian Papan, and Courtney Tsotich v. Pro-Football, Inc. Cancellation no. 92046185, Trademark Trial and Appeal Board, Patent and Trademark Office (P.T.O.). https://h2o.law.harvard.edu/cases/4667.

Amireh, Amal and Majaj, Lisa Suhair, eds. 2000. *Going Global: The Transnational Reception of Third World Women Writers*. Garland Reference Library of the Humanities, vol. 2194.

Anderson, Kim. 2011. *Life Stages and Native Women: Memory, Teachings, and Story Medicine*. Critical Studies in Native History, vol 15. Winnipeg: University of Manitoba Press.

Anzaldua, Gloria. 1990. *Making Face, Making Soul/Haciendo Caras: Creative and Critical Perspectives by Feminists of Color.* San Francisco: Aunt Lute Foundation Books.

Archibald, Jo-Ann, Jenny Lee-Morgan, Jenny, Jason De Santolo, and Linda Tuhiwai Smith. 2019. *Decolonizing Research: Indigenous Storywork as Methodology.* London: Zed Books.

Archuleta, Elizabeth. 2006. "I Give You Back:" Indigenous Women Writing to Survive. *Studies in American Indian Literatures* 18, no. 4 (Winter 2006): 95–114.

Barson, Benjamin and Gizelxanath Rodriquez. 2019. "Artivism and Decolonization: A brief Theory, History and Practice of Cultural Production as Political Activism," September 5, 2019. https://nmbx.newmusicusa.org/artivism-and-decolonization-a-brief-theory-history-and-practice-of-cultural-production-as-political-activism/.

Battiste, Marie. 2013. *Decolonizing Education: Nourishing Their Learning Spirits.* Sasakatoon, SK: Purich Publishing Ltd.

Begay, Cassandra. 2017. "Live Desk with President Barack Obama at Obama Foundation Summit in Chicago," November 1, 2017. https://www.youtube.com/watch?v=mlQt_mJmId8.

Berghof, Gwen. "Environmental Activist Winona LaDuke Shares a Powerful Message of Hope." *The Occidental,* October 29, 2019.

Beverley, John. 2004. *Testimonio: On the Politics of Truth.* Minneapolis: University of Minnesota Press.

———. 2000. "Testimonio, Subalternity, and Narrative Authority." In *Handbook of Qualitative Research.* 2nd ed, edited by Norman K. Denzin and Yvonna S. Lincoln. Thousand Oaks, CA: Sage Publications.

Blackwell, Maylei. 2015. "Geographies of Difference: Transborder Organizing and Indigenous Women's Activism." *Social Justice* 42, no. 3/4, p. 137–154.

Cabezas, Almudena. 2014. "Transnational Feminist Networks Building Regions in Latin America." *Latin American Policy* 5, no. 2, p. 207–220.

Cajete, Gregory A. 2011. Review of "Lois Meyer and Benjamin Maldonado Alvarado, eds.: New World of Indigenous Resistance: Noam Chomsky and Voices from North, South, and Central America." *The American Indian Quarterly,* March 22, 2011.

Chisom, Ronald, Michael Washington, and People's Institute for Survival Beyond. 1997. *Undoing Racism: A Philosophy of International Social Change.* New Orleans, LA: People's Institute Press.

Chúngara de Barrios, Domitila. 1977. *Let me Speak! Testimony of Domitila, a Woman of the Bolivian Mines.* New York: Monthly Review Press.

Cinnamon Kills First. https://www.cinnamonkillsfirst.com/publications.

Clacso, Premio Berta Cáceres. "La lucha de las mujeres por la igualdad en América Latina y el Caribe." https://www.clacso.org/la-lucha-de-las-mujeres-por-la-igualdad-en-america-latina-y-el-caribe-2/.

Clissold, Stephen. 1965. "The Indian Problem in Latin America: Changing Attitudes in the Andean Republics." *Race* VII, no. 1, p. 47–57.

Colectiva#SOS: Antiracismo, Género y Justica. "Irma Velásquez Nimatuj." https://www.colectivasos.com/integrantes/irma-velasquez/.

Coulthard, Glen Sean. 2014. *Red Skin, White Masks: Rejecting the Colonial Politics of Recognition.* Minneapolis: University of Minnesota Press.

Cultural Survival Quarterly. 2012. "A Decade of Cultural Survival Quarterly." https://www.culturalsurvival.org/publications/cultural-survival-quarterly/decade-cultural-survival-quarterly.

De la TorreAmaguaña, Luz Maria. 2015. "What Does It Mean to Be an Indigenous Woman in Contemporary Times?" Translated by Isabel Dulfano in. *Indigenous Feminist Narratives: I/We: Wo(men) of An(other) Way*. London: PalgravePivot.

Delgado, Pop A., Morna Macleod, and María Luisa Pérez-Armiñán Cabrera. 2000. *Identidad: Rostros Sin Máscara: Reflexiones Sobre Cosmovisión, Género Y Etnicidad.* Guatemala: Oxfam-Australia.

Díaz, Esther and Rivera Cuscicanqui, Silvia. "Algunas Consideraciones Para Una Ética Aplicada a La Investigación Científica." Retrieved September 28, 2019, from https://www.estherdiaz.com.ar/textos/etica_investigacion.htm.

Donna M. Loring Papers. Maine Women Writers Collection, University of New England, Portland, Maine.

Döring, Tobias. 2011. *Postcolonial Literatures in English*. Uni-Wissen Anglistik-Amerikanistik 4. Stuttgart: KlettLernen und Wissen GmbH.

Dulfano, Isabel. 2009. "Another Way of Envisioning the World." *Cultural Survival Quarterly*, December 2009.

Elsted, Jeff, ed. *We Shall Remain—The Navajo*. KUED, 2009. https://watch.opb.org/video/kued-local-productions-we-shall-remain-navajo/.

Ensler, Eve. 2001. *The Vagina Monologues*. Rev. ed. New York: Villard Press.

Everett, Jana Matson and Sue Ellen M. Charlton. 2014. *Women Navigating Globalization: Feminist Approaches to Development*. Lanham, Maryland: Rowman & Littlefield.

Fernández Benítez, Hans M. 2010. "The Moment of testimonio is over: problemasteóricos y perspectivas de los estudiostestimoniales." *Medellín, Colombia: Íkala, Revista de Lenguaje y Cultura* 15, no. 24 (Jan./Apr.), p. 47–71.

Ferree, Myra M., and Aili M. Tripp. 2006. *Global Feminism: Transnational Women's Activism, Organizing, and Human Rights*. New York: New York University Press.

FIAN International. "Crisanta Pérez." https://vimeo.com/79784711.

Finley, Taryn. 2018. "Viola Davis' Powerful Speech for Women of Color at the Women's March", *The Atlanta Voice*, January 26, 2018.

Fletcher, Matthew L. M. 2014. "A Short History of Indian Law in the Supreme Court." American Bar Association, 2014. https://www.americanbar.org/groups/crsj/publications/human_rights_magazine_home/2014_vol_40/vol--40--no--1--tribal-sovereignty/short_history_of_indian_law/.

Florio, Maria and Victoria Mudd, et al. 1985. *Broken Rainbow*. Los Angeles, CA: Earthworks Films, Inc.: Direct Cinema, Ltd [distributor]

FNX First Nations Experience. https://fnx.org/.

Fraser, Nancy. 2003. "Nuevas reflexiones sobre el reconocimiento." London: New Left Review, Vol. 4.

Freedom House. "Democracy in Crisis," Freedom House, November 21, 2017. https://freedomhouse.org/report/freedom-world/freedom-world-2018.

———. 2017. *Freedom in the World*. Washington, D.C.: Freedom House.https://freedomhouse.org.

Friederic, Karin. 2014. Review of "Feminist Activist Ethnography: Counterpoints to Neoliberalism in North America." In *American Ethnologist*, edited by Christa Craven and Dána-Ain Davis, Vol. 41, no. 4. Lanham, MD: Lexington.

Gatschet, Albert S. 1885. "The Beothuk Indians." *Proceedings of the American Philosophical Society* 22, no. 120. Philadelphia, 408–424.

Gehrke, S. "Utes Can Keep Their Name: NCAA Takes the U Off the List of Offending Schools." *Daily Utah Chronicle*, September 6, 2005. https://dailyutahchronicle.com/2005/09/06/utes-can-keep-their-name-ncaa-takes-the-u-off-the-list-of-offending-schools.

Global Witness. "Global Witness Reports 227 Land and Environmental Activists Murdered in a Single Year, the Worst Figure on Record," September 13, 2021. http://www.globalwitness.org/en/press-releases/global-witness-reports-227-land-and-environmental-activists-murdered-single-year-worst-figure-record/.

Gonzalez Prada, M. 1961. "Nuestros Indios." *Horas de lucha.* Secondedition (Callao: Tip. Lux, 1924; Translated by H. E. Davis, "Our Indians." *Latin American Social Thought.* Washington: The University Press of Washington.

Grossman, Zoltan. "Treaty Rights and Responding to Anti-Indian Activity." The Fourth World Documentation Project at The Center for World Indigenous Studies. Retrieved August 2018. http://www.dickshovel.com/anti.html.

Guerrero Arias, Patricio. 2010. "Corazonar El Sentido De Las Epistemologías Dominantes Desde Las Sabidurías Insurgentes, Para Construir Sentidos Otros De La Existencia (Primera Parte)." *Calle14: revista de investigación en el campo del arte*, vol. 4, no. 5. Bogotá, D.C.: Universidad Distrital Francisco Jose de Caldas.

Gugelberger, Georg M. 1996. "Introduction: Institutionalization of Transgression: Testimonial Discourse and Beyond." In *The Real Thing: Testimonial Discourse and Latin America*, edited by Georg M. Gugelberger. Durham: Duke University Press.

Gutiérrez Rodríguez, Encarnación, Manuela Boatcă, and SérgioCosta. 2010. *Decolonizing European Sociology: Transdisciplinary Approaches.* Farnham: Ashgate Publishing Ltd.

Hafen, P. Jane. 2020. "Help Indians Help Themselves:" The Later Writings of Gertrude Simmons Bonnin (Zitkala-S'a). Lubbock: Texas Tech University Press.

Hargreaves, Allison. 2017. *Violence Against Indigenous Women: Literature, Activism, Resistance.* Waterloo, ON: Wilfrid Laurier University Press.

Harjo, Suzan Shown. "Offensive Mascots Belong in Museums and History Books." https://www.indianz.com/News/2017/12/15/suzan-shown-harjo-offensive-mascots-belo.asp.

Hawkesworth, Mary. 2006. *Globalization and Feminist Activism.* Rowman & Littlefield Publishers, Lanham, Md.

Houska, Tara. 2018. "The Standing Rock Resistance and Our Fight for Indigenous Rights." TED Talks April 2018. https://www.ted.com/speakers/tara_houska.

Howe, John, producer and Ken Verdoia, director. 2009. *The Long Walk: Tears of the Navajo.* Salt Lake City: KUED-TV.

Huber, L. 2009. "Disrupting Apartheid of Knowledge: Testimonio as Methodology in Latina/o Critical Race Research in Education." *International Journal of Qualitative Studies in Education* 22, no. 6, p. 639–654.

"Indigenous Women Rising." *Cultural Survival Quarterly* 42, no. 1, 2018.

"J. Sales: Activists in Guatemala Branded Enemies of the State." *San Diego Union-Tribune*, August 30, 2016. https://www.sandiegouniontribune.com/en-espanol/sdhoy-jsales-activists-in-guatemala-branded-enemies-of-the-state2016aug30-story.html.

Jawort, Adrian L., ed. 2014. Off the Path: An Anthology of 21st Century Montana American Indian Writers, Vols. 1 & 2. Billings, Montana: Off the Path Press, LLC.

Johnson, David L. and Raymond Wilson. 1988. "Gertrude Simmons Bonnin, 1876-1938: 'Americanize the First American.'" *American Indian Quarterly* 12, no. 1, p. 27–40.

Juris, Jeffrey and Alex Khasnabish. 2013. *Insurgent Encounters: Transnational Activism, Ethnography, and the Political.* Durham, NC: Duke University Press.

Kaplan, Temma. 2001. "Uncommon Women and the Common Good." In *Women Resist Globalization: Mobilizing for Livlihood and Rights*, edited by Sheila Rowbotham and Stephanie Linkogle, vol. 28, no. 45. London: Zed Press.

Keeler, Jacqueline. 2017. *Edge of Morning: Native Voices Speak for the Bears Ears.* Salt Lake City: Torrey House.

King, Martin Luther. 1964. *Why We Can't Wait.* New York: New American Library, Harper & Row.

Klein, Naomi. 2013. "Dancing the World into Being: A Conversation with Idle No More's Leanne Simpson." *Yes!* March 6, 2013.

Klein, Rebecca. 2015. "Native American History Is Often Overlooked In Schools. One State Is Trying To Change That," *Huffington Post*, May 13, 2015.

Kovach, Margaret. 2009. *Indigenous Methodologies: Characteristics, Conversations, and Contexts.* Toronto, Canada: University of Toronto Press.

Krouse, Susan Applegate and Heather Howard-Bobiwash. 2009. *Keeping the Campfires Going: Native Women's Activism in Urban Communities.* Lincoln, NE: University of Nebraska Press.

LaDuke, Winona. 2014. "Minobimaatisiiwin - the good life." TEDxSitka, July 20, 2014. www.youtube.com/watch?v=pPJ3nrsCcrE.

———. 2016. *Recovering the Sacred: The Power of Naming and Claiming.* Chicago: Haymarket B ooks.

———. 2012. "Seeds of Our Ancestors, Seeds of Life." TEDxTC, March 4, 2012. www.youtube.com/watch?v=pHNlel72eQc.

———. "Vice Presidential Campaign Discussion." Winona LaDuke papers, Coll 372, Special Collections & University Archives, University of Oregon Libraries, Eugene, Oregon.

Las Casas, Bartolomé, del. 1875. *Historia De Las Indias.* Fuensanta, V. F. R. A., and Rayón J. L. Sancho. Madrid: Imprenta de Miguel Ginesta.

Lewandowski, Tadeusz. 2017. *Zitkala-Sa: Letters, Speeches, and Unpublished Writings, 1898-1929.* Leiden, Boston: Brill.

Limerick, Patricia Nelson. 1987. *The Legacy of Conquest: The Unbroken Past of the American West.* New York: W. W. Norton.

Living Justice Press. "Profile: Elizabeth Cook-Lynn." https://livingjusticepress.org/elizabeth-cook-lynn/.

Lloyd, T. G. B. 1875. "On the 'Beothucs,' a Tribe of Red Indians, Supposed to Be Extinct, Which Formerly Inhabited Newfoundland." *The Journal of the Anthropological Institute of Great Britain and Ireland* 4, p. 21–44.

Loring, Donna M. 2008. *In the Shadow of the Eagle: A Tribal Representative in Maine.* Maine: Tillbury Press.

Lui, Meizhu. *The Color of Wealth: The Story behind the U.S. Racial Wealth Divide.* New York: New Press.

Macleod, Morna. 2011. *Nietas del fuego, creadoras del alba: Luchas político-culturales de mujeres mayas.* Guatemala: FLACSO.

Maier, Elizabeth and Nathalie Lebon, eds. 2010. *Women's Activism in Latin America and the Caribbean: Engendering Social Justice, Democratizing Citizenship.* New Brunswick, N.J.: Tijuana, Mexico: Rutgers University Press; El Colegio de la Frontera Norte A.C.

Maier, Linda S. and Isabel Dulfano. 2004. *Woman as Witness: Essays on Testimonial Literature by Latin American Women.* NY. London: Peter Lang.

Mariátegui La Chira, José Carlos. 1928. *7 Ensayos de interpretación de la realidad peruana.* Lima: Biblioteca Amauta.

Means, Russell. 1980. "For the World to Live, Europe Must Die," *Mother Jones.* Winona LaDuke papers, Coll 372, Special Collections & University Archives, University of Oregon Libraries, Eugene, Oregon.

Menchú, Rigoberta. 1983. *I, Rigoberta Menchú, An Indian Woman in Guatemala.* London: Verso.

Meyer and Benjamin Maldonado Alvarado, eds. 2010. *New World of Indigenous Resistance: Noam Chomsky and Voices from North, South, and Central America.* San Francisco: City Lights Books.

Miles, Nelson A. "The Indian Problem." *The North American Review* 128, no. 268, March 1879, 304–314. *Jstor.* www.jstor.org/stable/pdf/25100734.pdf?refreqid=excelsior %3Adf4f781c696bb248b0ec19f69fa0c561.

Mitchell, Sherri L. and Larry Dossey. 2018. *Sacred Instructions: Indigenous Wisdom for Living Spirit-based Change.* Berkeley, CA: North Atlantic Books.

Nandy, Ashis. 1983. *The Intimate Enemy: Loss and Recovery of Self Under Colonialism.* Delhi: Oxford University Press.

Naples, Nancy A. and ManishaDesai, eds. 2010. *Women's Activism and Globalization: Linking Local Struggles and Global Politics.* Oxford: Routledge.

New York Times. "Obituary," 1934. National Council of American Indian Records, 1926–1938 MSS 1704, L. Tom Perry Special Collections, Brigham Young University Libraries.

Ouellette, Grace J. M. W. 2002. *The Fourth World an Indigenous Perspective on Feminism and Aboriginal Women's Activism.* Halifax: Fernwood Publishing.

Palmater, Pamela. 2011. *Beyond Blood: Rethinking Indigenous Identity.* Vancouver, British Columbia: University of British Columbia Press, Purich Publishing.

———. 2019. Keynote Speech, Ethnicity, Race, and Indigenous Peoples Conference, Gonzaga University.

———. 2020. *Warrior Life: Indigenous Resistance and Resurgence.* Black Point, Nova Scotia: Fernwood Publishing Company, Ltd.

Perez Huber, Lindsay. 2009a. "Challenging Racist Nativist Framing: Acknowledging the Community Cultural Wealth of Undocumented Chicana College Students to Reframe the Immigration Debate." *Harvard Educational Review* 17, no. 4(Win), p. 704–729.

———. 2009b. "Disrupting Apartheid of Knowledge: 'Testimonio' as Methodology in Latina/o Critical Race Research in Education." *International Journal of Qualitative Studies in Education* 22, no. 6 (Nov), p. 639–654.

Pratt, Richard H. 1973. "The Advantages of Mingling Indians with Whites." *Official Report of the Nineteenth Annual Conference of Charities and Correction. 1892.* Reprinted in *Americanizing the American Indians: Writings by the "Friends of the Indian" 1880-1900.* Cambridge: Harvard University Press.

Prensa. 2021. *Entrevista: Antonia Benito: Alzar la voz desde la comunicación comunitaria*, FGER-Federación de Guatemala de Escuelas Radio Fónicas, November 25, 2021.

Presley, Rachel. 2020. "Embodied Liminality and Gendered State Violence: Artivist Expressions in the MMIW Movement." *Journal of International Women's Studies* 21, no. 7. p. 91–109.

Quijano, Anibal. 2000. "Coloniality of Power, Eurocentrism, and Latin America." In *Nepantla*, no. 3. Durham, North Carolina: Duke University Press.

Rechtshaffen, Michael. 2017. "Review: Powerful '500 Years' Doc Concludes Trilogy on Guatemalan Resistance," *Los Angeles Times*, July 27, 2017.

Reporters Without Borders, World Press Freedom Index, "United States Rank 2017," November 12, 2017. https://rsf.org/en/ranking/2017.

Robles, Barbara J., Betsy Leondar-Wright, Rose Brewer, Meizhu Lui, and Rebecca Adamson., 2005. *The Color of Wealth: The Story Behind the U.S. Racial Wealth Divide.* New York: The New Press.

Robles Lomeli, Jofte Dilian and Joanne Rappaport. 2018. "Imagining Latin American Social Science from the Global South: Orlando FalsBorda and Participatory Action Research." *Latin American Research Review* 53, no. 3, 597–612.

Sale, Kirkpatrick. 1991. *The Conquest of Paradise: Christopher Columbus and the Columbian Legacy.* New York: Knopf, 1990; New York: Plume, 1991.

"Samantha Eldridge." George Washington College of Professional Studies. https://cipp.cps/gwu.edu/samantha-eldridge.

Schoolcraft, Henry. "BIA Policy Recommendation." Rebecca Adamson papers, Sophia Smith Collection of Women's History, Smith College.

Sempértegui, Andrea. 2019. "Indigenous Women's Activism, Ecofeminism, and Extractivism: Partial Connections in the Ecuadorian Amazon." *Politics & Gender*, 17 (1) p. 197–224.

Simpson, Audra, et al. 2014. *Mohawk Interruptus: Political Life Across the Borders of Settler States.* Durham, North Carolina: Duke University Press.

Simpson, Leanne Betasmosake. 2017. *As We Have Always Done: Indigenous Freedom through Radical Resistance.* Indigenous Americas. Minneapolis: University of Minnesota Press.

———. 2016. "Indigenous Resurgence and Co-Resistance." *Journal of the Critical Ethnic Studies Association* 2, no. 2, p. 19–34.

Sitkala-Sa. *Americanize the First American: A Plan of Regeneration. Library of American Indian Affairs.* National Council of American Indian Records, 1926–1938, MSS 1704, L. Tom Perry Special Collections, Brigham Young University Libraries.

Sittig, Ann. 2009. "Contemporary Guatemalan Mayan Women Write an Identity Based on Respect, Interconnectedness, Love and Peace." *Letras Femeninas* 35, no. 2, p. 153–172.

Smith, Linda Tuhiwai. 1999. *Decolonizing Methodologies: Research and Indigenous Peoples.* London: ZED Books, Ltd; Dunedin, New Zealand: University of Oswego Press.

Speed, Shannon, et al. 2006. *Dissident Women: Gender and Culture Politics in Chiapas.* Austin: University of Texas Press.

Spivak, Gayatri Chakravorty and Rosalind C. Morris. 2010. *Can the Subaltern Speak: Reflections on the History of an Idea.* New York: Columbia University Press.

Stephen, Lynn and Speed, Shannon. 2021. *Indigenous Women and Violence: Feminist Activist Research in Heightened States of Injustice.* Tucson: University of Arizona Press.

Stephen, Lynn. 2007. *Transborder Lives: Indigenous Oaxacans in Mexico, California, and Oregon.* Durham, North Carolina: Duke University Press.

Steinberg, Stephen. 2007. *Race Relations: A Critique.* Stanford: Stanford University Press.

Steiner, Stan. 1968. *New Indians.* New York: Harper & Row.

Stinchcombe, Arthur Leonard. 1984. "The Origins of Sociology as a Discipline." *Acta Sociologica* 27, no. 1, p. 51–61.

Taliman, Valerie. 2002. "Sacred Landscapes." *Sierra Club*, November/December 2002.

Thompson, Lucy. 1991. *To the American Indian: Reminiscences of a Yurok Woman.* Berkeley: Heyday Books.

Trafzer, Clifford E., et al. 2021. *Indigenous Activism: Profiles of Native Women in Contemporary America.* Lanham: Lexington Books.

Transparency International. "Corruptions Perceptions." 2016. https://www.transparency.org/en/cpi/201.

Tubin, Victoria. "Ser mujer y ser maya." *Plaza Publica*, March 25, 2015. https://www.plazapublica.com.gt/content/ser-mujer-y-ser-maya.

Tuck, Eve and Marcia McKenzie. 2015. "Relational Validity and the 'Where' of Inquiry: Place and Land in Qualitative Research." *Qualitative Inquiry.* Sage Publications.

Tujal, Juana Batzibal, et al. 2000. *Identidad: Rostros sin máscara: Reflexiones sobre cosmovisión, género y etnicidad.* Oxfam-Australia.

———. "Juana Batzibal, Universidad Estatal a Distancia (UNED)." https://redinterculturalidad.wordpress.com/2014/08/15/conversatorio-mujer-indigena-y-educacion-con-juana-batzibal-lider-indigena-de-la-etnia-maya-kaqchikel-de-guatemala-y-antropologa-video/.

———. 2018. "Mujer Indígena y Educación: Una Mirada Desde La Visión De Juana Batzibal, Indígena Maya Kaqchikel." UNED. Mujer Indígena y Educación, Auguest 6, 2018, Costa Rica, www.uned.ac.cr/acontecer/a-diario/sociedad/2124-mujer-indigena-y-educacion-una-mirada-desde-la-vision-de-juana-batzibal-indigena-maya-kaqchikel.

———. 2009. "Mujeres indígenas y justicia ancestral." In *Conflictos por herencias de mujeres en la justicia ancestral*, compiled by Miriam Lang Anna Kucia. Ecuador: UNIFEM 2009 FLACSO.

Unspoken: America's Native American Boarding Schools. Salt Lake City: KUED, 2016. https://www.pbs.org/video/unspoken-americas-native-american-boarding-schools-oobt1r/.

Velásquez Nimatuj, Irma Alicia. 2016. "Indigenous Women and Activism." Public Lecture, The University of Utah.

———. 2015. “Memory/Memoir, Challenges and Anthropology.” In *Indigenous Feminist Narratives: I/We: Wo(men) of An(other) Way*, translated by Isabel Dulfano. London: Macmillan; Palgrave Pivot.

Winona LaDuke papers, Coll 372, Special Collections & University Archives, University of Oregon Libraries, Eugene, Oregon.

Zitkala Sa. “America’s Indian Problem,” *A Celebration of Women Writers*, November 20, 2016. http://www.digital.library.upenn.edu/women/zitkala-sa/stories/problem.html.

Zuberi, Tukufu. 2001. *Thicker Than Blood: How Racial Statistics Lie.* Minneapolis: University of Minnesota Press.

Zuberi, Tukufu and Eduardo Bonilla-Silva, eds. 2008. *White Logic, White Methods: Racism and Methodology*. Lanham: Rowman & Littlefield.

Index

A

B

C

G

H

I

J

K

L

O

P

Q

R

S

T

U

V

W

X

Y

Z

CRITICAL INDIGENOUS AND AMERICAN INDIAN STUDIES

Andrew Jolivette
General Editor

The Critical Indigenous and American Indian Studies series welcomes highly innovative, inter-disciplinary manuscripts that explore the historic and contemporary experiences of American Indians, Alaska Natives, and Indigenous Peoples throughout Oceania and the Pacific. We seek submissions from scholars working on the following topics: literary studies, community/public health, languages and cultural preservation, cultural studies, gender and sexuality, politics and sovereignty, religion and philosophy, education, and media studies. This series seeks to increase the international presence of scholarly monographs written and published by American Indian and Indigenous Peoples that address indigenous people's rights as a matter of social justice and human rights.

For additional information about this series or for the submission of manuscripts, please contact:

editorial@peterlang.com

To order books, please contact our Customer Service Department:

peterlang@presswarehouse.com (within the U.S.)
orders@peterlang.com (outside the U.S.)

Or browse online by series at:

www.peterlang.com

www.ingramcontent.com/pod-product-compliance
Lightning Source LLC
Chambersburg PA
CBHW070551100726
47907CB00004B/1342
* 9 7 8 1 4 3 3 1 9 7 3 8 3 *